Amerindian Legends of Guyana

by
Odeen Ishmael

Artex Publishing, Inc

Copyright © 1995 by Odeen Ishmael

All rights reserved. No part of this publication may be reproduced or transmitted in any form or by any means, electronic or mechanical, including photocoping, recording, or by any information storage and retrieval system, without the written permission of the author, except where permitted by law.

ISBN-0-930401-87-5
Library of Congress Catalog Card Number: 95-79103

Artex Publishing, Inc.
P.O. Box 976
Sheboygan, WI 53082

DEDICATION

*This book is dedicated
to my wife, Evangeline,
my son, Waseem,
and my daughter, Nadeeza.*

ACKNOWLEDGEMENT

Some of the sketches that illustrate this book are based on photographs or pictures which might have appeared in other publications. The author wishes to express the appropriate acknowledgement to any such publication.

Amerindian Legends of Guyana

Contents

INTRODUCTION - 7
1. HOW THE FIRST PEOPLE ARRIVED ON EARTH - 13
2. THE WONDERFUL TREE - 16
3. THE FLOOD - 21
4. WHY THE ALLIGATOR HATES OTHER ANIMALS - 24
5. THE FIRST CARIB - 26
6. HOW THE SUN PRINCE MARRIED USIDIU - 32
7. MAKONAIMA AND PIA - 36
8. HOW MAKONAIMA AND PIA MET THEIR FATHER - 39
9. WHY THERE ARE STORMS ON MOUNT RORAIMA - 42
10. BOONA, MAYOROKOTO AND TIGER - 48
11. THE LEGEND OF HABURI - 53
12. THE LEGEND OF THE HAIARRI ROOT - 58
13. THE MAN WHO LIKED TO BOAST - 60
14. THE YOUNG HUNTER AND THE MAGICIAN'S DAUGHTER - 62
15. THE OLD MAN'S WATERFALL - 66
16. THE GIRL WHO WAS ONCE A MONKEY - 70
17. THE WAR OF THE BIRDS - 74
18. THE ADVENTURES OF KOROROMANNA - 78
19. THE ORIGIN OF THE CALABASH - 87
20. THE STORY OF AMALIVACAR - 91
    GLOSSARY - 96
    FURTHER READING - 101

— Introduction —
The Amerindians of Guyana

The Republic of Guyana, a British colony up to 1966, is a relatively small country of 83,000 square miles (216,000 square kilometers) located on the northern shoulder of South America. The population which currently is approximately 800,000 is made up of at least six ethnic groups. Roughly 85 percent of this total live on the narrow coastal plain bordering the Atlantic Ocean. This coastal plain, while being very low, is extremely rich in its fertile alluvial soils.

The remaining 15 percent of the population live in scattered villages in the interior, which is thickly forested, except for an area of savannah near the Brazilian border. It is a country full of hills and mountains, interspersed with thousands of rivers and creeks.

Among the people who live in the interior forests and savannah are the Amerindians, who comprise about 5 percent of the country's population. The name Amerindian is coined from two words — American Indian — to differentiate those people from the East Indians whose ancestors were brought from India by the British colonials during the nineteenth century to work, and, later to settle in the country. At the present time, East Indians make approximately 51 percent of Guyana's population.

Amerindians were the original inhabitants of Guyana. Some historians claim that ethnic group has been living in the country for more than 12,000 years. Traditionally, the Amerindians, who are Mongoloid in appearance, have been forest dwellers, depending on hunting, fishing and simple agriculture for food. Their agriculture has always been primitive, and they are still applying their slash and burn method today, probably because of the poor agricultural soils in the areas where they live.

Amerindian Legends of Guyana

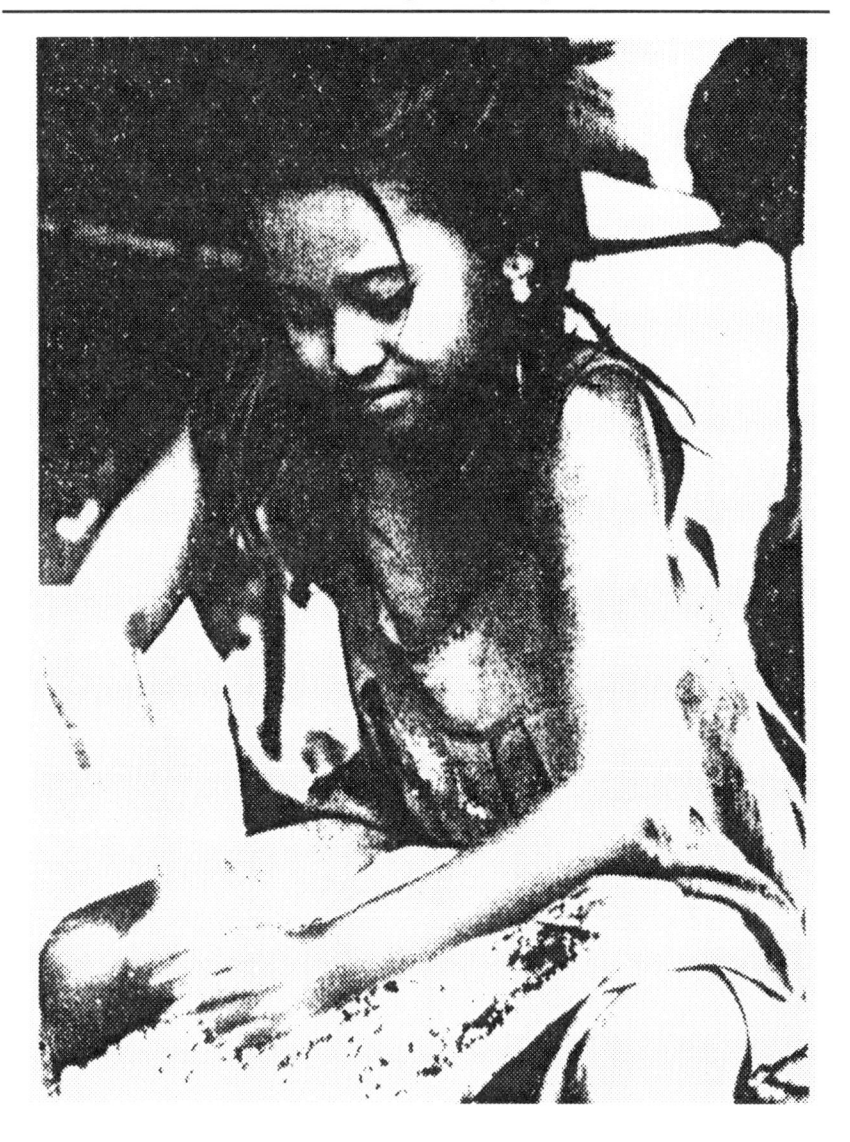

Amerindian girl grating cassava

Their villages are still located close to rivers and creeks, which, in addition to being routes on which they travel in canoes, are important for fishing, bathing and fresh water.

Historians claim that at the time when Columbus came to the American continent in 1492, there were an estimated 70,000 Amerindians in Guyana. However, after centuries of tribal warfare, migration to neighboring countries, plantation slavery, and culture shock from the clash with European civilization, their numbers were drastically reduced to 7,500 by 1891. Since then there has been an upsurge in population growth, and today, the Amerindians number almost 40,000.

The Amerindian population is divided into nine tribal groups — Arawak, Arecuna, Akawaio, Carib, Makushi, Patamona, Wai-Wai, Wapishana and Warrau. Tribal divisions are based on different languages, and, to a lesser extent, on cultural traditions.

Traditionally, each tribe has occupied specific geographical areas. However, with modern technology and culture, including airplanes and motorboats for traveling, guns for hunting, radio and formal education, tribal divisions are clouded in many areas. This is complicated by intermarriage between the tribes, the nearly universal use of the English language at the expense of tribal languages, and the almost complete conversion of Amerindians of all tribes to Christianity by missionaries. Also of importance is the creation by the Makushi, Akawaio and Carib tribes of an indigenous religion known as *Hallelujah* which is heavily based on Christianity, but incorporates elements of those tribes' traditional beliefs, too.

Significantly, most young people of all tribes, almost all of whom have received at least six years of formal education in schools, either do not communicate in the tribal language or have totally forgotten it. Further, the Amerindians have been absorbed into Guyanese society. They no longer have a primitive outlook. Traditional clothing of loincloths and beads is hardly ever worn, because modern clothing is the trend. While some have achieved relatively very high levels of modern education and are now teachers, nurses, civil servants, and members of parliament, the areas in the interior where the Amerindians still live remain the least economically developed parts of the country.

At present, the Amerindians have adopted a money economy and have moved away almost entirely from the traditional bartering system. In some areas almost all able-bodied men work on the *timber grants* for several months of the year. During that time, women and children tend the farms. In the Rupununi savannahs near the Brazilian border, Amerindian men work as *vaqueros* on the large cattle ranches. Some are gold miners and *balata bleeders*. *Balata* is the natural rubber formed from the sap of the bulletwood tree.

Even though their subsistence farms produce a variety of fruits, vegetables and root crops, *cassava* remains the main produce and the chief item on the Amerindian diet. Although there are two main types of cassava — sweet cassava and bitter cassava — the Amerindians cultivate the bitter variety, which has poisonous acids in the juice.

When the cassava is grated, squeezed in a *matapee* to remove the cassava juice that contains the poison, dried, sifted, roasted, fermented and processed in many other ways, they produce a variety of foods, including cassava bread, *farine, casseri* and *paiwarri.* In addition, *casareep,* a preservative sauce, is made from the juice through a process of steady boiling to neutralize the acids.

The contribution of the Amerindians to Guyanese society is noteworthy. One of the by-products from the processing of bitter cassava is a dish known as *pepper-pot*, made from *casareep*, meat and hot pepper. The dish has become national and is very popular among all ethnic and cultural groups.

In addition, the making and use of the hammock, the identification and use of innumerable medicinally valuable indigenous plants, the manufacture and use of the drug *curare*, the domestication and "education" of the parrot — Amerindians first taught it to speak — and the naming of many of the country's rivers, mountains, flora and fauna, all come from the ingenuity of Amerindians.

Very little is known of Amerindian history in Guyana before

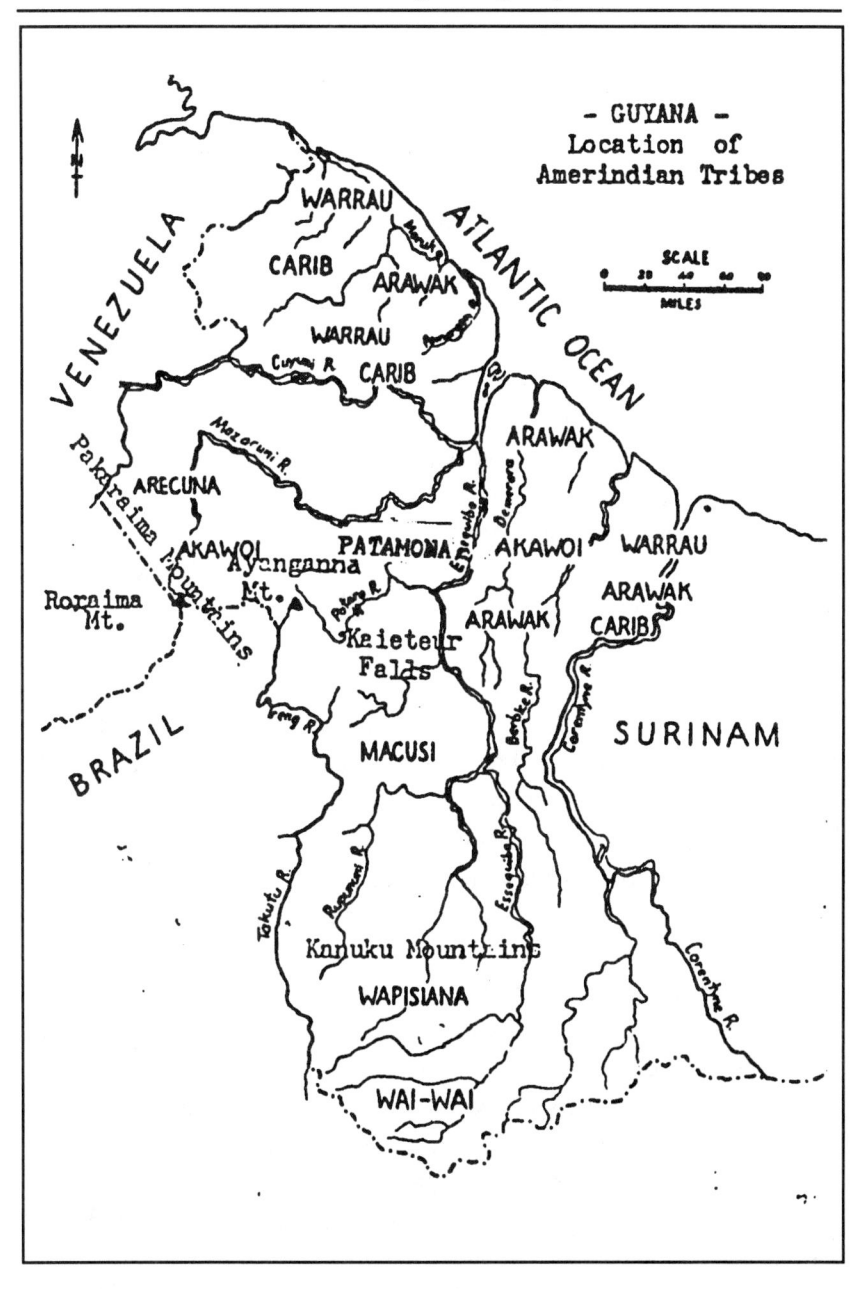

Map of Guyana showing the location of Amerindian tribes

the arrival of European settlers in the early seventeenth century. No written form of their languages existed until recently. Much of the history that is known is based on oral traditions which are not quite clear, because the periods when important events occurred are difficult to place.

Still, native oral traditions are very rich in folk stories of the ancestral heroes and heroines of the Amerindian people. There are different versions of some stories among the different tribes. Such a difference is illustrated in this book — the Warrau version of the legend of Makonaima and Pia is given in three stories, *How the Sun-Prince Married Usidiu, Makonaima and Pia,* and *How Makonaima and Pia Met Their Father.* The Makushi version is told in *Why There are Storms on Mount Roraima.*

The above points about the Amerindians' culture and economic development are mentioned to give the reader some background against which to place the stories in this collection.

The present set of Amerindian legends materialized over a period of more than ten years during which the author listened to versions of these legends from Amerindian adults. Significantly, most of these legends have also been summarized since the late nineteenth century, by a succession of researchers, including Everard F. im Thurn, W.H. Brett, Walter Roth and Leonard Lambert.

The author has also been in contact with some Amerindian children who know these stories, but their narrative is affected by changes in technology. Instead of the hunter hero using a bow and arrow, these children see him using a gun.

Despite such adulteration, the stories the author heard formed the basis for the stories in this collection.

An important character in Amerindian legends is Tiger. There are many tigers and, generally, they are villains. However, there are no tigers in Guyana or on the entire American continent. What is generally referred to is the large spotted jaguar, which Guyanese call a tiger.

The author has found the twenty stories in this collection particularly interesting. He hopes his readers will feel the same.

1
How The First People Arrived On Earth

A long, long time ago, there were no human beings on Earth. At that time, a group of people known as the Warraus lived in Skyland and they did not know Earth existed.

One of the Warrau men, Okonorote, was a very famous hunter. Whenever he set out to hunt he always returned with something. Furthermore, if he followed a deer or a bird, he never gave up the chase until he killed it. He chased his prey for days until he was finally able to shoot it with his bow and arrow.

One day, Okonorote was in the forest and saw a fat wild turkey. He decided he would not rest until he shot it. The turkey was very agile and led him on a tiresome chase for many days. Finally, Okonorote was able to hit it with his sharp arrow and knock it from its perch high in the treetops.

When the bird fell, it went into a deep pit on the forest floor. Okonorote was determined to have that turkey. He had not chased it for all those days just to leave it in a hole. He knelt beside the hole, and peered down to see where the turkey landed. To his surprise, he saw a strange land far below where many animals walked lazily about.

After gazing at this scene for a long time, Okonorote hurried toward home. When he arrived at the village, his tribesmen gathered around him and were very surprised.

"Okonorote," an old man asked, "where's the animal you were hunting?"

"This is the first time you ever came home empty-handed!" another man said.

Okonorote looked at them and then said, "My friends, it's true I have returned home empty-handed for the first time, but I followed a wild turkey for many days. When I finally shot it, it fell into a deep hole in the forest floor. I looked into the hole to find the turkey and saw a strange land at the bottom where many animals grazed. I saw no human beings there."

"Take us to this hole," a young man said.

"Let us go," Okonorote replied.

Okonorote, followed by all the men and older boys of his village, returned to the hole in the forest.

"Look into the hole and tell me if I haven't spoken the truth," he said.

One by one, they looked, and it was as Okonorote said — they saw hundreds of animals living on the strange land at the bottom of the hole.

All the men of the village were hunters, and their mouths watered when they saw those animals. They wanted to get down there so they could have meat all year round, but they did not know how to reach that land.

Okonorote solved the problem. "Let's weave a long rope from all these bushes growing here. We can tie one end to that tree trunk, and we'll drop the rest down the hole. I'll then climb down the rope to the land below. When I'm ready to come up, I'll tug the rope twice, and you can haul me up."

They worked quickly. Soon a long rope was woven and dropped down the hole. Okonorote, armed with his bow and arrow, climbed down swiftly. After a while, he stepped onto the strange land.

The first thing he did was look for the turkey, which he found laying on some soft grass. He was amazed at the richness of the land and at the large number of animals that lived in it. Seeing a deer grazing nearby, he shot it and set it beside the turkey. That was the first deer he ever saw — Skyland had no such animal.

He tied the deer and turkey to the rope, tugged twice, and held on firmly. Far above, his friends felt the tugging and they quickly pulled him up.

Later that day, they butchered the deer and shared it with all the families in the village. The meat was so tasty that everyone, including the women and children, felt that they, too, should go to the strange land to hunt more deer.

The next morning, all the villagers — men, women and children — began to climb down the rope to the new land.

Then disaster struck.

A very fat woman managed to reach halfway through the hole and then got stuck. Those who had already arrived in the new land tugged on the rope in an effort to free her, but she remained stuck. Those still in Skyland climbed down into the hole in an effort to remove the woman, but it was impossible. Finally, everyone gave up.

Ever since, the Warraus who had arrived in the new land — which was really the Earth — were forced to remain there. Those in Skyland had to stay where they were, too. They are probably still there. And because the fat woman still blocks the hole linking Earth and Skyland, no one on either side has been able to know what is happening to those on the other side.

The fat woman who blocks the hole cries bitterly sometimes. When she does, her tears fall to the Earth as rain.

2
The Wonderful Tree

Long, long ago, the forest spirit, Tamosi, made a tree that produced almost all the different useful fruits and vegetables. The tree looked like all the other trees in the forest, and it was left there for people or animals to discover and use.

Some time after people began living on Earth, Maipuri, the tapir, found the strange tree by accident. He was surprised to see the different kinds of fruits and vegetables hanging from its branches. This was the first time he saw many of them.

"This tree will feed me the rest of my life," Maipuri said.

After he ate as much as he could, he went back to the village at the edge of the forest where he lived with other animals among the people.

At that time there was a famine, and there was very little food available, not only for people, but for animals, too. Even in the rivers and creeks there were hardly any fish to be caught to be used for food.

Maipuri, who was very selfish, decided not to tell anyone of the wonderful tree he had found. With the food shortage, he would have to share the fruits and vegetables growing on the tree.

"If I tell the animals and human beings of this tree," he reasoned, "all will reap the fruits. After a while, I won't get enough to eat."

Every day Maipuri went deep into the forest to the wonderful tree. After stuffing himself like a glutton, he returned to the village in the evening. With all the food he was eating, he soon became very fat.

The people of the village noticed how Maipuri was getting fatter.

"Where are you getting food, Maipuri?" they asked. "You're being very selfish if you have food and keep it all to yourself."

"Just because I'm getting fat doesn't mean I've found food," he replied. He walked away from the villagers and other animals and went to his home so he could sleep.

"Let's send some men to follow him in the morning," the villagers said. "Maybe he's got food in the forest. If the men follow him, they'll be able to see where he gets his food and bring some back for us."

The next morning, five young men set out quietly behind the tapir. But Maipuri saw them and slipped between some thorn bushes. The thorns did not harm him because he had tough skin, but the men were forced to give up following him. They went back to the village and told everyone how Maipuri escaped.

"Now we know he's got food in the forest," one of the young men said. "Otherwise, he wouldn't have slipped away from us. If we can follow him secretly, I'm sure we can find the source of his food."

The villagers discussed other means of following the tapir. One old man suggested, "Let's send Woodpecker to follow him. Woodpecker will fly in the air, and Maipuri won't see him."

Everyone agreed to that, and, the next day, Woodpecker flew quietly and followed the tapir into the forest. But Woodpecker could not resist tapping on trees along the way. Maipuri heard the steady tapping behind him and realized that Woodpecker was following him.

"So they've sent Woodpecker to follow me," he chuckled. "I know how to fool him."

Suddenly, Maipuri ran away from the track through the bushes until he came to an area with many dead trees. There were countless worm holes on the tree trunks. Hiding under nearby bushes, Maipuri watched Woodpecker fly toward the trees.

The bird could not resist and started tapping at the worm holes. Maipuri knew that Woodpecker would not leave the area until he finished checking all the holes.

Smiling to himself, Maipuri moved away quietly to the magic tree, where he had a wonderful meal. In the evening, when he was returning home, he heard Woodpecker tapping at the dead trees.

Late that night Woodpecker returned to the village and re-

Maipuri, the tapir

ported his failure to follow Maipuri.

After another discussion, the villagers decided to send Rat after Maipuri. Rat was a good choice. He was small and very quiet when he moved.

The next day, Rat followed Maipuri to the magic tree. Maipuri lay under the tree and chewed a mouthful of cassava when Rat came up.

"So this is where you get your food," Rat said. "You're very selfish and greedy. Don't you want others to enjoy the fruits the way you do?"

"Look, Brother Rat," replied Maipuri, "If I show this tree to everyone, in no time all the fruits will be eaten. Why don't we keep this secret together? Then only the two of us will enjoy these tasty fruits?"

Rat was also a selfish animal, and he readily agreed to Maipuri's suggestion. He sat beside Maipuri and stuffed himself with as much corn as he could eat for a week.

Late that evening he returned to the village. "I'm sorry, but Maipuri was too clever for me," he told the villagers. "I lost his track in the forest and, after trying for hours to find it, I gave up and decided to come home."

Every day the villagers and other animals watched Maipuri growing fatter and fatter. No one ever suspected Rat. He was sly enough to slip away to the tree at night to eat.

One morning, Rat overslept. He was tired and had returned home just before daybreak. He was so tired he fell asleep on his doorstep and snored with his mouth open. Stuck to his teeth were a few grains of corn!

Sigu, the old fisherman, saw the grains of corn and called the villagers, who angrily shook Rat awake.

"You were fooling us!" they shouted. "Where did you get the grains in your mouth?"

"I won't tell you," Rat yelled back.

"If you don't tell us we'll feed you to Cat," Sigu said quietly.

Rat trembled. He was terribly afraid of Cat, so he quickly

revealed the secret he and Maipuri kept. Then the people forced him to lead them to the magic tree deep in the forest.

What a wonderful tree it was! On its branches, the people saw plantains, bananas, cassava, yams, corn, papayas and fruits and vegetables of all kinds.

The people and animals who came with them ate like gluttons and finally fell asleep under the tree's shady branches. When they awoke, they were surprised to see a strange old man standing nearby.

"Who are you?" they asked.

"I am Tamosi, the forest spirit," he replied. "I planted this tree."

"We're sorry we ate without your permission," Sigu said.

"Don't be sorry," the forest spirit replied. "I planted this tree for all humans and animals to have fruits when they need them, but I don't want anyone to be selfish like Maipuri and Rat. Everyone must have a share. I want you cut down the tree and divide the branches equally among all of you. Plant the branches in your own plots, and you will have all the fruits and vegetables that you need."

For many weeks afterward, the people of the village cut at the thick tree trunk with their stone axes. Eventually, the tree fell, and they cut away the branches and divided them among themselves. Then they planted the branches in their gardens.

From those branches came all the different plants. Some time later, people reaped cassava, sweet potatoes, corn, bananas, papayas and many other fruits and vegetables.

As for the selfish Maipuri and Rat, they were so ashamed of themselves they moved away into the forest and lived alone.

3
The Flood

A few months after the magic tree was cut down, Sigu, the old man who had made the final chop of the trunk, returned to the place where the tree once stood. To his surprise, he found the stump was hollow down the middle. Inside was water, and he saw young fishes of all kinds swimming there.

"Why are all these little fishes here?" he wondered.

After considering the matter for a few minutes, he said, "I know what I'll do. I'll put the fishes in the streams and rivers around here."

For many months, Sigu traveled throughout the land to distribute the little fishes in the various rivers and streams. After he finished, he went back to the tree trunk for a final look.

He was shocked to see that the water in it was overflowing, streaming steadily out onto the ground. He quickly made a *warrampa*, a basket woven from reeds, and covered the stump with it. This sealed the hole, forcing the water to remain inside the tree trunk.

In a village in another part of the forest, Iwarrika, the monkey, was caught stealing corn from a farm. He was taken before the village elders and, after being put on trial for his misdeed, the chief elder told him, "For stealing corn, you will be badly punished. This is your punishment — you must fetch water from the river and fill the empty duck pond. However, you must fetch the water with a basket."

Iwarrika fetched water for months with a reed basket. It, of course, leaked almost all the water he tried to carry. To make his many trips to the river more interesting, he followed different tracks through the forest.

One day, he found the tree trunk Sigu covered with his *warrampa*. Iwarrika stopped and wondered why there was an upside down *warrampa* on the tree stump.

"I'm sure that someone must have hidden a lot of fruits under it," he said.

He snatched away the *warrampa*, but, instead of fruits, a heavy stream of water rushed out from the hollow tree trunk. With a scream, Iwarrika ran off, but the water overtook him and drowned him in the flood.

Soon, the forest floor was covered with water that kept rising. Not long after that, even the villages were covered by the rising flood.

There was great panic in Sigu's village. Some people ran away, while others headed for the distant mountains. Most of those were overtaken by the water and drowned.

But Sigu did not panic. He gathered all the animals that could not swim and locked them in a cave with a narrow entrance. After leaving the animals a thin thorn, he sealed the entrance from outside with bees' wax.

"Every day," Sigu said, "bore a tiny hole through the wax with the thorn. By looking through the hole, you can check the water level."

Sigu then climbed the tallest *cookrit* palm and made himself comfortable among the top branches. All the birds and the beasts that could climb also went up the palm tree to stay with him. After a while, the flood came near the level of the branches, then stopped rising.

For many weeks, Sigu lived in the branches of the *cookrit* palm tree with the birds and beasts. Every morning he dropped a seed from the palm tree to check the level of the flood. With the passing of time, the animals on the tree top grew impatient, and the red howling monkey roared so loudly that his throat swelled. Ever since, howling monkeys have swollen throats.

Eventually, the flood receded, and land could be seen again. Sigu and the birds and animals decided it was time to climb down. Immediately after they did, Sigu hurried to the cave and released the animals locked inside.

Sigu and his animal friends were not the only survivors of the flood. The others were Marerawara and his family.

Marerawara lived near the Cuyuni River. He was very kind-hearted and helped people in need. No one who went to his house for cassava or sweet potatoes was ever turned away.

The same could not be said of the others living in his village. They were very quarrelsome and stole other people's crops at night.

One night, Marerawara had a strange dream in which he saw the village covered by water. He regarded his dream as a sign and told people of his fears.

"The whole land will be flooded," he said. "We must prepare for it."

But they laughed at him in scorn.

"You're a dreamer! Why don't you leave us alone?" they mocked at him.

Nevertheless, Marerawara believed his dream. He tied a strong bush rope to his big canoe, anchoring it to a tall tree near his home. He placed himself, his wife, his four children, and several of animals he raised into the canoe. For food, he stocked dried meat and many kinds of fruits.

As soon as he finished his preparations, the flood waters that drowned Sigu's village reached Marerawara's village. The flood rose rapidly, and the canoe rose with it. Soon, the other villagers drowned.

After many weeks, the water subsided, and the canoe eventually settled back to the ground. Marerawara, his wife, his four children, and his livestock climbed out and began their task of building their home all over again.

4
Why The Alligator Hates Other Animals

When the great flood ended, all the birds and beasts that were with Sigu on the *cookrit* palm, climbed down to solid land.

The trumpet bird was in a great hurry. He was hungry after missing his regular meals which he usually obtained from the forest fruits. He did not look where he was going, and he landed on top of a ball of red-ants which had floated in the flood.

The ants were hungry, too, and they clung to the trumpet bird's meaty legs. In almost no time, the bird's legs were reduced to a thin bony shape. To this day trumpet birds have thin bony legs.

Sigu was hungry, too, and he immediately began to prepare a meal. He rubbed two pieces of wood together to make fire. The first spark flew off the wood, and the turkey, thinking it was a firefly, flew up and swallowed it. Of course, it burned his throat. Trying to spit it out, he made a strange sound — "Gobble, gobble." All turkeys make that sound to this day. The heat from the spark also formed red lumps on the turkey's throat and, ever since, all turkeys have those red lumps.

Sigu did not see the turkey swallow his spark. He looked around for it but he could not find it anywhere. Just then, he saw Alligator in the nearby stream looking at him. At once, he suspected that Alligator saw the spark and swallowed it.

Sigu turned to the other animals around him and asked, "Who stole the spark?"

No one knew the turkey swallowed it, so they said, "Alligator stole the spark."

Sigu believed them and became very angry. He jumped into the stream, grabbed the innocent Alligator, and tore out his tongue, but he never found the spark.

From that day, Alligator has hated all other animals for the lie they told against him. He still has a small tongue, and he attacks the other animals whenever they come near.

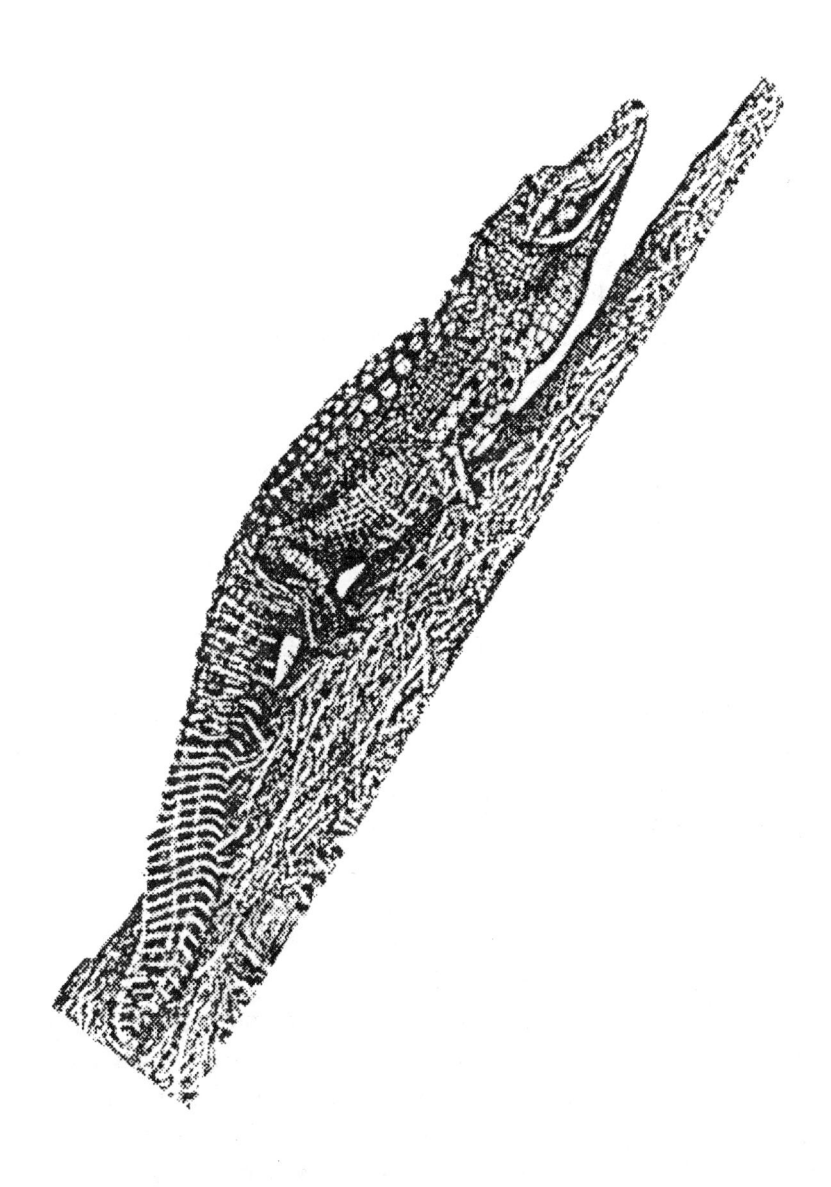

The alligator

5
The First Carib

Deep in the forest, there was a quiet lake on the shores of which was a Warrau village. From that lake, the Warraus got water for drinking, while the abundant fish that thrived there gave them food.

But no one was allowed to swim in the lake. When the children asked why, the old men said, "A long time ago, the Great Spirit told our people to drink the water and catch the fish, but we were never to swim in the lake. Our grandparents and our parents obeyed that law, and you must obey it, too. If you don't, bad things will happen to you."

That satisfied the young people, and no one used the lake for anything but fishing and collecting drinking water. All swimming was done in the river that fed the lake. There was peace, and everyone was happy.

Very near the lake was a house in which eight persons lived. They were Koroma and Koroko, a father and mother, four brothers named Kororoma, Kororomana, Kororomatu and Kororomatitu, and two sisters named Korobona and Korobonako.

These brothers and sisters were told repeatedly not to swim in the lake, but the two young women were curious and secretly decided to swim there to see if anything would happen.

Many years before, in the middle of the lake the magicians of the Warraus planted an old tree trunk that would protect the people from the powers of the Water Spirit that lived at the bottom of the lake. If anyone touched that tree trunk, all the magic powers in it would disappear, and there would be no control over the Water Spirit. This was the real reason no one was allowed to swim in the lake. However, all of this was unknown to the people who lived near to the lake.

Early one morning, the curious sisters, Korobona and Korobonako, quietly slipped from the house before dawn and plunged into the lake and swam about in the cool refreshing water.

"This is beautiful!" Korobona said.

"Yes," replied Korobonako. "It's stupid for the old people to keep us from enjoying themselves in the lake."

"Let's race to that old tree trunk," shouted Korobona.

She swam off, with her sister swimming closely behind.

Korobona was the first to reach the tree trunk. She grabbed it and shook it vigorously. Immediately, the spell controlling the Water Spirit was broken. The Water Spirit took the form of a man and jumped to the surface of the lake near the tree trunk. He snatched Korobona and took her to his home under the surface of the lake.

Terrified, Korobonako swam back to the shore and hurried home to tell her parents and brothers what happened.

Meanwhile, in the Water Spirit's home, Korobona was terribly afraid and expected to be put to death at any moment.

"If you become my wife," the Water Spirit said, "You'll be safe. One day, you can return to your people."

"What will happen if I refuse?" asked the frightened girl.

"You die immediately," the Water Spirit answered.

She agreed to live with the Water Spirit and be his wife. After some time passed, she gave birth to a son, but he was very strange. He was beautifully formed, but the lower part of his body, from the waist down, was that of a *camudi* snake!

A few weeks after the birth, the Water Spirit told Korobona, "You will now go back with our child to your home above the lake. If, at any time, you need my help, all you have to do is to shake the tree trunk in the middle of the lake."

Korobona swam to the surface with her strange child, and set out toward her parents' home.

By this time, everyone in the village thought Korobona died. Her family was very surprised when she walked through the door. They were even more surprised to hear her story, and her parents quickly forgave her for breaking the village law about swimming in the lake.

"At least the Water Spirit won't annoy us," her parents said.

"He is our son-in-law."

However, her brothers would not forgive her. "No, she must go away," they declared. "She has brought disgrace upon us for not obeying the law of our people."

But her parents insisted that she had to live with them. They explained, "She is our daughter. Her child is our grandson."

Her brothers grumbled. They had to accept their parents' decision, but they refused to speak to Korobona. Her sister, Korobonako, however, helped her care for the child.

One night, the four brothers plotted quietly to kill the child, but Korobona overheard their whispers and suspected they were planning something against the child. After her brothers fell asleep, she slipped out of the house and hid her child in the forest.

Every day, she went to her secret hiding place to feed him, but her visits could not remain secret for long. One day, her brothers followed her to the hiding place. Korobona had just finished feeding her baby and played with him on the grass under the tall trees, when her brothers arrived. They shot the baby with arrows and ran off.

Korobona quickly pulled out the arrows and treated her son's wounds with juices from plant leaves that grew around the hiding place. The child recovered and, after a few months, grew into a huge half-man, half-snake.

At first, her brothers thought that they killed the child, but, after they saw Korobona still slipping away into the forest, they realized that their plan failed.

Again, they followed her into the forest and were astounded to see the size of her son. They went home and prepared many arrows and other weapons so they could kill him. They acted as if they were making ordinary hunting weapons. But when Korobona saw the vast amount they were producing, she realized her brothers must have followed her into the forest again and saw that her son was still alive.

She had to warn her son of the danger. She slipped away from the house and ran into the forest. Nevertheless, her brothers were watching her and grabbed their weapons to follow her.

When her son crept out from his hiding place to greet her, the brothers arrived and fired arrows at him in showers. He was severely injured and lay helpless on the ground.

Seeing him that way, the four brothers jumped on him, and, in the presence of the weeping mother, chopped him into little pieces.

"He is dead now!" they shouted as they ran off.

Korobona wept over her son's mutilated remains for hours. Finally, she covered the pieces of his body with heaps of green leaves and walked sadly toward the lake. She plunged into the calm water and swam to the tree trunk sticking out in the middle of the lake. She grasped it with both hands and shook it hard.

Immediately, her husband, the Water Spirit, was beside her.

"What is the matter, Korobona?" he asked.

"Our son is dead," she told him. "My brothers shot him with arrows. When he was helpless, they chopped him into little pieces. I want revenge."

"Go back to where the body lies," the Water Spirit told her. "Keep watch over it, and soon, you shall have your revenge."

Korobona swam back to shore and returned to the place where her son's body lay. She stared at the pile of leaves covering the body, and cried bitterly all day.

Then, as evening approached, she saw that the leaves began to shake as if a living creature was under them. Out of the pile of leaves rose a huge, handsome warrior, fully human. In his hands he held his bow and arrows, and he was dressed for battle.

He looked at Korobona and whispered, "My dear Mother, you will have your revenge. My name is Carib. I'll drive away those who have tormented us."

Leaving her standing there, he rushed through the forest and attacked his uncles and all other Warraus who came to their aid. No one could stand up to Carib. He quickly killed his wicked uncles and drove the other Warraus before him.

Later, he returned to his mother. For a while, he lived happily with her, his aunt, and his grandparents on the bank of the peaceful lake. The most beautiful of the Warrau maidens became his wife, and his children became strong, brave warriors like himself.

The first Carib

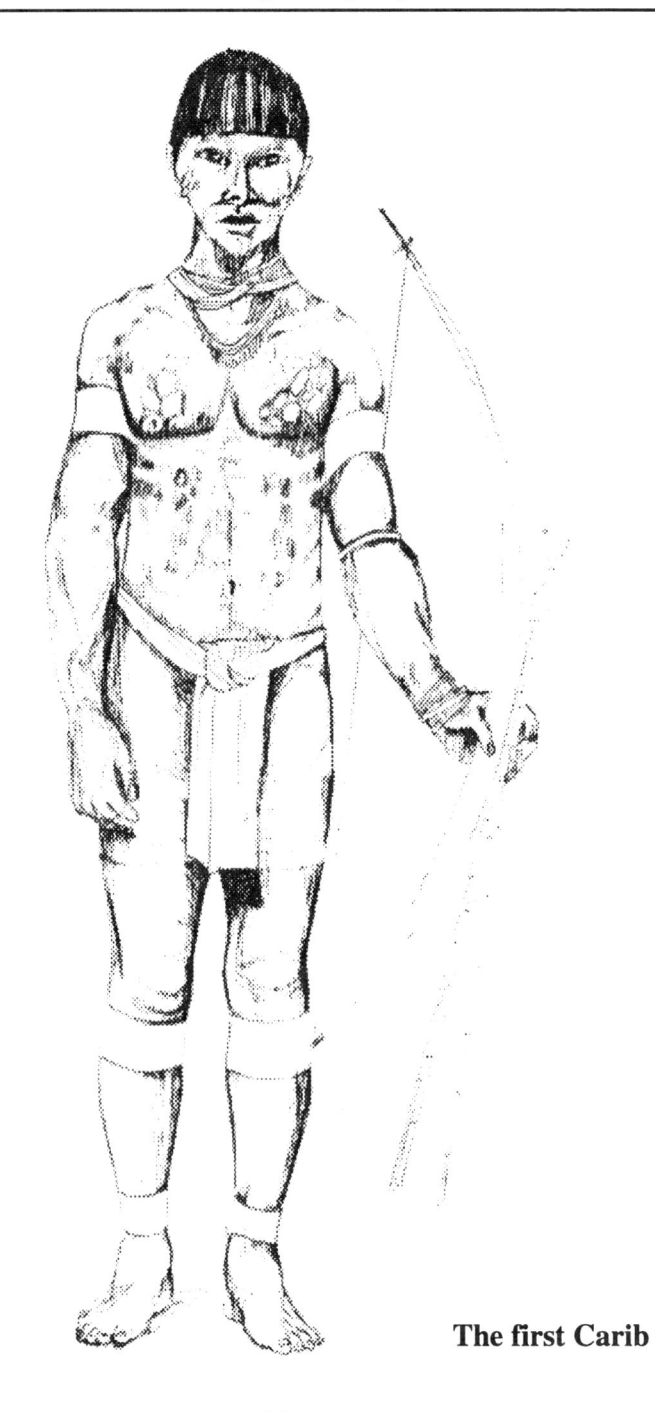

In a relatively short time, a fierce Carib tribe grew up and lived on the bank of that lake. Later, when the Warraus tried to regain their homes and land Carib originally seized, the fierce Carib tribe drove them to the muddy shores of the Atlantic Ocean and took full possession of the Warraus' rich hunting grounds in the forest.

6
How The Sun Prince Married Usidiu

Long, long ago, an old magician named Nahakaboni lived in the forest. He had a beautiful daughter named Usidiu. She was kind, pleasant, and hard-working, and was loved by all the people and the animals that lived in the forest.

One day, while Usidiu was fetching water from the river, the Sun Prince saw her and fell in love with her. He made a vow that this was the girl he was going to marry.

The next morning, the Sun Prince went to Nahakaboni's home and asked for Usidiu to be his wife.

"Nahakaboni," he said, "I saw your beautiful daughter by the river yesterday, and if I don't marry her, I will surely die."

Usidiu was listening in another room, and she peeked through a hole in the wall. She saw the handsome Sun Prince and immediately fell in love with him. She hoped that her father would agree to his request.

Nahakaboni loved his daughter very much, and he told himself repeatedly that she must be married to someone who would perform difficult tasks. He said to the Sun Prince, "I will agree to let her marry you only if you show you are capable of doing three difficult things. Only if you perform those deeds will you prove that you can care my daughter."

"Oh, Nahakaboni," replied the Sun Prince, "I am willing to carry out your wishes."

"Here is your first task," said the old man. "I want you to fetch water from the river with my basket and fill the big clay pot standing behind the house."

The Sun Prince was amazed at this request, but he nevertheless picked up the reed basket and walked down the forest path to the river.

No matter how many times he dipped the basket in the water, it all ran out the moment he lifted the basket. He wondered what to do.

Usidiu, upon hearing her father's task for the Sun Prince, knew that he would not be able to collect water with the basket unless she helped him. She, like her father, could perform magical deeds.

She quietly climbed through the window of her room and ran to the river. There she saw the Sun Prince trying in vain to fill the basket with water.

Seeing her, he asked, "What can I do, Usidiu? It seems that I may not be able to have you for my wife."

"Let me touch the basket," she said.

He held up the basket, and she lightly touched it with her fingers. It immediately changed into a basket made of skin — without any holes! The Sun Prince was now able to fetch water and fill the huge clay pot.

When the task was completed, Usidiu, who hid near the big pot, touched the basket and changed it back to its original form.

The Sun Prince returned to Nahakaboni and handed him the basket. "The pot is filled," he announced.

The old man quickly examined the filled pot and looked sharply at the Sun Prince. "Someone must have helped you. But your next task will be more difficult. Bring my fishing arrow which is in my canoe. The canoe is in the river."

The Sun Prince thought that sounded easy, so he rushed to the river bank where Nahakaboni's canoe was tied to a stump. To his surprise, he saw an alligator lying across the canoe, while a large snake lay curled up at the bottom.

He was very afraid of alligators and snakes, and he dreaded going near the canoe. Just then, Usidiu appeared in the bushes beside him.

"What can I do?" he asked. "It seems I can't carry out the second task."

She smiled and tossed a pebble into the canoe. The alligator changed into a canoe seat, and the snake turned into a fishing arrow. The Sun Prince hurriedly picked up the arrow and took it to Nahakaboni.

The Sun Prince and his wife

"Someone must have helped you," Nahakaboni declared. "For your final task, you have to shoot the big *lukanani* fish in the river. However, you must shoot your arrow into the air and have your back to the river when you do it."

The Sun Prince felt the last task was hopeless. Everyone knew the big *lukanani* was a magical fish, and that the only way it could be killed was in the manner the old man had described. Many skilled hunters and fishermen tried to kill it in the past, but all failed.

Nevertheless, the Sun Prince gathered his bow and arrows and walked slowly toward the river. He was not a skilled hunter, and he wondered how he could shoot the fish without aiming at it in the water. Furthermore, how could he kill it by shooting into the air? How was he to know in which part of the river the fish was?

But Usidiu was waiting for him by the river bank with an arrow in her hand. "Take this magic arrow and fit it to your bow," she explained. "Turn your back to the river and shoot the arrow above your head. But make sure that your eyes are closed."

The Sun Prince did as she told him. He waited a few seconds after he shot the arrow, and he hesitantly opened his eyes. To his amazement, he saw the *lukanani* floating on the surface of the river with his arrow in its side. He leaped into the water, grabbed the fish, and swam back to the river bank. Then he gave Usidiu back the magic arrow and she ran through the bushes to her home.

Shortly after, he took the fish to Nahakaboni.

"My dear Sun Prince," the old man said, "either someone helped you, or you yourself have powerful magic. I will keep my promise and give you my daughter as your wife."

There was great rejoicing among the forest people as they and Nahakaboni celebrated the wedding of the Sun Prince and the beautiful Usidiu.

7
Makonaima And Pia

After the Sun Prince and beautiful Usidiu married, they lived in their home by the riverside. Early one morning, the Sun Prince told Usidiu that he was going to hunt in the forest.

"My dear wife," he said, "don't leave the house. You'll give birth to our child at any time now."

She promised to remain inside, then she stood by the door and waved goodbye to him. She watched him walk through the woods until he disappeared in the darkness of the forest.

While her husband was away, Usidiu kept busy by cleaning the house and mending clothing. At noon, she discovered that her husband forgot to take the meal that she prepared for him to eat during the hunt. The neatly wrapped parcel of dried meat and *farine* was still on the kitchen table.

Thinking that he would be hungry, she picked up the parcel and set out along the narrow pathway into the forest. There were many more pathways in the forest, and, after following some and shouting her husband's name without luck, she decided to return home.

But no matter how much she tried, she could not find the way out of the forest. In despair, she realized she was hopelessly lost.

Usidiu made many attempts to get out of the forest, but every time she followed a new path, she just moved deeper into the forest. As night approached, she saw a little hut among the trees. Her spirits lifted, for she felt that she would get help from whoever lived there.

She tapped on the door she called out, "Please help me. I'm lost in the forest."

The door opened, and an old woman stepped out. "My name is Nanyoba," she croaked. "Come into my hut and rest. You look weak, hungry, and ill."

Usidiu entered the hut. After seating herself on a low stool, she told Nanyoba how she ended up in the forest.

"My dear girl," said the old woman, "I've lived my entire life in this forest, and I myself don't know the way out. But I'm sure your husband will search for you. He'll find you safe here."

She gave Usidiu a meal of boiled sweet potatoes and a cup of *casseri* to drink. Shortly after Usidiu ate, she felt ill.

"I feel ill. I'm about to give birth."

That evening she gave birth to twin boys. However, she was so ill and weak that she fell unconscious. Nanyoba tried to help her, but Usidiu died late that night, when the moon was high above the trees.

Nanyoba was a wicked witch, and she always wanted children who would work for her. She decided to keep the twins and make them believe that she was their mother.

Early the next morning, she buried Usidiu in a hole she dug behind the hut. After feeding the twins on cassava milk, she named them Makonaima and Pia.

Two days later, the Sun Prince came to Nanyoba's hut and asked if she saw his wife. "I haven't seen anyone for two months," Nanyoba replied.

Makonaima and Pia grew quickly. By the time they were sixteen years old, they were handsome youths, skilled in hunting and fishing. By then, too, they realized that they had magical powers. They did not know that they inherited those from their mother.

They also sensed that there was something mysterious about Nanyoba.

"She never cooks with fire for us to see," Makonaima told Pia. They became determined to see how the old woman cooked meals for them.

One morning, Nanyoba sent the boys to collect firewood. Shortly after they left the hut, Makonaima changed himself into a lizard and climbed up the wall to an open window. He was amazed to see the old woman spitting fire and swallowing it again.

He changed back to himself and ran to Pia to tell him his

discovery.

"She's a witch!" Pia exclaimed. "We have to kill her. She's evil."

"I don't think she's our mother," Makonaima said. "She never wants to talk about our father."

During the night, the boys slipped from the hut and piled dry branches around it. They set it on fire and burned Nanyoba in the flames.

But the old witch did not die. She changed into a frog with scorched and wrinkled skin.

It is said that as she burned, the fire she kept in her body jumped out of her mouth and hid in a *hima-heru* tree that grew nearby. Today, if two *hima-heru* sticks are rubbed together, they quickly produce fire.

8
How Makonaima And Pia Met Their Father

After burning Nanyoba, Makonaima and Pia decided to search for their father. Since they did not know their real mother, they knew that finding their father would be very difficult.

As they roamed in the forest, they met people and animals and asked them if they knew anything about their parents. Everyone they met said, "No, I do not know who your parents are."

One afternoon, the boys shot two *powis* with their bows and arrows, intending to cook them for dinner.

"These aren't enough," Pia said. "Let's shoot another."

Just then, they saw another *powis* on a nearby tree. As Makonaima aimed his arrow at it, the bird spoke. "Please don't shoot me! If you spare my life, I'll tell you about your parents."

Makonaima was excited. "I promise to spare your life and the lives of all *powis* in the future if you do."

The grateful bird told the boys of their parents' marriage and how their mother died after they were born.

"Your father is alive," the bird told them. "He lives on the edge of the forest on the riverbank. He grieves for your mother, Usidiu, and also for the child or children she expected to have. He can't have her back, but he will be happy to have both of you, even though he doesn't know you."

"How will he know us?" asked Pia.

"That is easy," replied the bird. "Makonaima, you look like your father, while you, Pia, are the image of your mother."

"Thank you very much, *Powis*," the boys said. "We will go to meet our father now."

The crested powis

After many days of walking, they arrived at the edge of the forest. There on the riverbank was the Sun Prince. He was a middle-aged man by then, sitting on a log near his house and gazing on the river's flowing waters.

"Father!" they shouted.

The Sun Prince turned. There was no mistaking the boys. One was the striking image of Usidiu and the other looked just as he himself was in his younger days.

"You are my sons!" he exclaimed, and embraced them warmly.

"Yes, Father," they replied happily.

Afterwards, they told their father about how Usidiu died and how they did not know about their parents until just a few days before. They also told him about their life with Nanyoba.

In turn, he told them of his search for Usidiu through the forest and how Nanyoba fooled him. He was very sad to hear of his beloved wife's death. "I will always love your mother, and even though she is dead, I have both of you to remind me of her," he told his sons.

Makonaima and Pia remained with their father. Soon, all the people around regarded then as the greatest hunters in the land.

9
Why There Are Storms On Mount Roraima

Many years ago, the Sun King entered the business of rearing fish. He made many fish ponds on Earth and occasionally visited them to catch the fish. However, while he was away, people or wild animals raided the ponds, so he never caught a satisfactory amount for himself.

After one of his trips to his fish ponds, he employed Yamuri, the lizard, to keep close watch on his ponds. But Yamuri was very lazy and loved to sleep in the sun. While he slept, people and the forest animals stole fish from the ponds.

The Sun King was very annoyed with Yamuri and told him that he no longer wanted to employ him.

The Sun King then went to the home of Alligator.

"Alligator, I want to employ you as watchman to take care of my fish ponds," said the Sun King.

"Why do you think I'd be a good watchman?" asked Alligator.

"Well, you see, you can swim in the ponds and when thieves come, you'll be there to catch them," explained the Sun King.

Alligator agreed to take the job, and the Sun King left feeling pleased that he had found a capable watchman.

But Alligator liked the taste of fish so much that he became the worst thief that ever robbed the ponds.

When the Sun King came to Earth to fish, he found his ponds had even less fish than before. And there in the middle of a pond was Alligator — with a fish in his mouth!

The Sun King was very angry. "You're the worst of thieves!" he yelled at Alligator and slashed at him with his *cutlass*. Every part of Alligator's body that received a cut formed a scar that looked like

Amerindian Legends of Guyana

The iguana

a large scale. To this day, all alligators bear those marks.

Alligator ran away to the swamps to nurse his wounds. He was terrified of the Sun King. To beg the king's forgiveness, he sent his cousin, *Iguana,* with a message.

Iguana traveled to the Sun and told the Sun King, "Alligator is very sorry for eating your fish. To pay you back, he offers his daughter as your wife."

By then, the Sun King's temper had cooled. A few days earlier, his sister, the Moon Princess, had told him that it was time for him to get a wife to care for him. Alligator's offer, therefore, suited him very well.

"Tell Alligator that I will accept his daughter," he told Iguana. "But that doesn't mean he's allowed near any of my fish ponds."

Iguana took back the news to Alligator, who became very worried. He never expected the Sun King to accept his offer, for he had no daughter to give him! What could he do?

Gradually, Alligator formed a plan. He carved a wild plum tree into the shape of a woman and begged the Water Spirit to breathe life into it. This the Water Spirit did, and Alligator immediately sent his new daughter to the Sun King.

Unfortunately, Alligator's ability to carve was extremely poor, and his daughter was indeed very ugly. Alligator knew that, and he feared that the Sun King would be very angry with him for sending such an ugly girl. Because of this, he hid in the swamp peeking out at the Sun to see if the Sun King was looking for him. To this day, all alligators still peek out at the Sun from the rivers and streams.

The Sun King was displeased with Alligator's ugly daughter, and, after living with her for a few months, he left her and never came back. But she loved the Sun King so much that she returned to Earth and searched for him.

After many weeks of searching, she still could not find her husband. Late one afternoon, she arrived at Mother Toad's house deep in the forest.

"What are you doing here?" Mother Toad asked.

"My husband, the Sun King, left me. I'm searching for him,"

replied Alligator's daughter.

"You won't find him," said Mother Toad. "When he wants to hide, no one ever finds him."

The girl began to cry very loudly, making Mother Toad feel sorry for her.

"Why don't you live with me?" Mother Toad asked.

The girl considered that for a while, then nodded. "My husband doesn't want to live with me. It might be best if I stay away from him and live with you."

At the time when she went to live with Mother Toad, the Sun King's wife was pregnant. Soon after she moved in with Mother Toad, she gave birth to twin boys, whom she named Makonaima and Pia. They were as handsome as their father.

The boys grew up under their mother's care at Mother Toad's home. Through their natural ability, they became very skilled hunters and fishermen.

One day, Mother Toad's son, *Tiger*, who lived in another part of the forest, came to visit. That was the first time he saw the twins and their mother.

When he about to leave, Tiger asked the twins' mother to marry him. She refused, and he became angry. With a roar, he jumped at her, slapped her heavily, and then ran away. She fell unconscious, and if it were not for the proper care she got from her sons and Mother Toad, she would have died.

After a few weeks, she recovered and was able to do her work in the home again.

Her sons developed a strong hatred for Tiger. One afternoon, as they hunted, they shot him with their poison arrows. Tiger did not die immediately. The poison made him suffer from terrible pains for three days before he finally died.

One day, Makonaima told his mother, "Pia and I are old enough now to be on our own. It's time I leave Mother Toad's house and travel throughout the land. I'd like Pia and you to accompany me."

She and Pia agreed, and after saying farewell to Mother Toad, they set out on a journey through the forest. On the bank of a large river, Makonaima cut down a big *crabwood* tree and shaped it into a canoe so they could travel on the numerous rivers.

During the course of their travels, Makonaima and Pia developed a new way to catch fish. They removed large boulders from the riverbanks and placed them in the river's swift waters. The rocks blocked the flow and kept the fish from moving downstream. Once the fish were all crowded up near to the rocks, the boys were able to shoot many of them which they cooked for their meals. Unfortunately, after making their catch, they did not bother to remove the rocks, which caused huge rapids and waterfalls to form.

Because of the large amount of fish Makonaima and Pia caught, Crane, the tall, long-legged bird, followed them very closely for leftovers. Soon he and the brothers became close friends, but this friendship eventually led to a serious quarrel.

Pia accused Crane of eating too much of the fish they caught. But Makonaima defended Crane, saying that this was not true. Eventually, the quarrel became so bitter that the two brothers separated and went their own ways. Makonaima took Crane with him when he left.

Pia and his mother remained together. He looked after her by supplying her with meat, fish and fruit. When she became old, he took her to the summit of Mount Roraima and built a hut for them. At certain times, Pia left the home and went to the villages on the lowlands to teach the people useful things. Later, all the learned men who went about teaching others became known as *piamen*.

Finally, Pia left the villages and returned to his mother on Mount Roraima.

"Mother," he told her, "I have finished my work of teaching the people all they must know. Now I shall leave you to go to another place far away to teach others. I won't return again, but I won't leave you without anything. If you ever need something, all you have to do is bow your head, cover your face with your hands, and wish for whatever it is."

Pia left his mother after bidding her a fond farewell.

To this day, his mother remains on Mount Roraima. She still

makes her wishes, but, when she thinks of her two sons and husband who deserted her, she becomes sad and cries bitterly. When that happens, there is a rainstorm on the mountain. Her tears form into streams that run down the steep slopes to join the rivers that flow through the forest to the great Atlantic Ocean.

10
Boona, Mayorokoto and Tiger

Once there was a beautiful girl who lived alone in a little house in a village near the forest. Her name was Boona. Her parents died a few years before, and, even though some of the people of the village wanted her to live with them, Boona preferred living by herself in her little house. She cultivated her own little farm on the edge of the forest some distance from her home. She often caught fish from the nearby creeks. Other villagers sometimes gave her meat from animals they killed in the forest.

One afternoon, Boona went to her farm to uproot some cassava. She saw that her farm was full of weeds, and, after she collected the cassava, she began clearing away some of the weeds. It was getting late, and she decided to return the next day to finish the task.

Early the next morning she returned to her farm. To her amazement, all the weeds were gone, and fresh cassava sticks, to generate new plants, were planted in the places where she uprooted cassavas the previous day.

"There is a very kind person here," she said to herself. "I'll be very glad to meet and thank that person."

From that day on, Boona's farm was always neat. Weeds were removed the moment they sprouted, plants were watered, and, when it was reaping time, the cassavas or sweet potatoes were neatly heaped up in a corner of the farm.

Boona never knew who did all that work. Even though she spent many entire days at her farm, she never found out who her helper was.

After giving some thought to these mysterious happenings, Boona concluded that her helper must come at night to work. She, therefore, decided to spend a night at the farm to see if she could discover who it was. After spending an entire day at the farm, she hid in a clump of bushes on the edge of the farm and waited.

At about midnight she heard leaves rustle. Out of the bushes stepped a handsome young man. Boona watched him walk to where sweet potatoes had recently been harvested. Very quietly, he shaped the sweet potato beds, and, as soon as he was finished, he planted sweet potato *slips* in them.

Boona stood and walked from her hiding place. The young man spun around when he heard her approaching footsteps.

"So you are the mysterious person who's been doing all the work on my farm," Boona said.

"Yes, Boona. I never wanted you to know," the young man replied.

"I must thank you very much. You have helped me a great deal. How can I thank you for all you've done?" asked Boona.

"I don't need any thanks. I've been doing all this because I have secretly loved you for a long time. My name is Mayorokoto, and I live in another part of the forest. We've never met. If you really wish to thank me, you can agree to be my wife," replied the young man.

Boona agreed, and a few days later they were married. They lived together in her little house, and they worked on the farm during the day. In time, they had a son they named Haburi.

But one day the happiness of this family was shattered. On that day, Mayorokoto left home early in the morning to fish. After trying for many hours, he could not catch any.

"Today must be a bad day for fishing," he said. "I know what I'll do. I'll fish in Tiger's creek."

True, there *was* a creek nearby that actually belonged to Tiger, and it was full of fish, but people were afraid to fish there. Boona had often warned Mayorokoto not to fish in Tiger's creek, but that morning he did not heed her warning. He went to Tiger's creek, and he was busy placing *haiarri* roots in the water to stun the fish, when Tiger leaped from the bushes. Two heavy slaps that he delivered on Mayorokoto killed him instantly.

Amerindian Legends of Guyana

The jaguar — the Guyanese tiger

Amerindian Legends of Guyana

Tiger dragged the body of the dead man to the bank and collected the stunned fish floating in the water. He packed them in the *quake* that Mayorokoto had brought with him.

Tiger looked at the Mayorokoto's body and laughed loudly, "So you were the husband of the beautiful Boona. I've always wanted her for my wife. Since you are dead, I'll take your place."

Tiger had magical powers and he changed himself into a man who looked exactly like Mayorokoto. Then he picked up the *quake* full of fish and went to Boona's house.

Boona was busy in the kitchen, baking cassava bread, when the disguised Tiger entered the house. The baby, Haburi, was creeping on the floor and was crying at the time.

"Mayorokoto," Boona called, "I know you're tired, but please look after Haburi until I'm finished in the kitchen."

Tiger picked up the baby and sat in Mayorokoto's hammock. Soon he fell asleep and began snoring very loudly.

Boona was shocked because her husband never snored loudly before. Meanwhile, Tiger was dreaming of how he killed Mayorokoto. Suddenly, he shouted in his sleep, "Mayorokoto, I killed you. Boona is my wife now!"

Boona heard him and became very frightened. She knew that was not her husband in the hammock. The voice was Tiger's. He must have killed Mayorokoto and used magic to take his shape.

She had to escape with Haburi. Moving quietly, she removed Haburi from Tiger's arms and substituted in them a bundle of cotton. She slipped from the house with Haburi and ran toward the house of Wowta, the old witch, her nearest neighbor. Still, she lived quite some distance away.

Shortly after Boona left, Tiger woke. He saw he was holding a bundle of cotton, not the baby. He realized that Boona knew who he was, so he changed back to his original shape, and rushed out of the house in time to see Boona running toward Wowta's house with the baby. He roared and raced after them.

Boona reached Wowta's house and screamed, "Wowta, open the door and let me in. I'm trying to escape from Tiger."

From inside, the old witch shouted back, "No, I don't want anyone coming in my house."

Boona heard Tiger roaring behind her. She turned and saw him rushing toward her. Suddenly, she got an idea. She pinched Haburi, who began to cry very loudly. Wowta opened the door in a flash. "Come in," she said, "I don't like hearing babies cry."

Boona rushed inside with the baby and slammed the door. "Thank you, Wowta. Please save me from Tiger," she begged.

Tiger was at the door. "Wowta," he shouted, "I want Boona and her baby. Put them outside immediately."

Wowta never liked Tiger. In addition to being a bully, he knew magic, and she was jealous of anyone else who practiced magic. "Boona and her baby are not here!" she shouted.

"I saw them enter the house," Tiger screamed.

Wowta opened the door slightly and said to Tiger, "If you don't believe me, push your head through the door and see for yourself."

The edge of the door was lined with sharp thorns. As soon as Tiger pushed his head through the small space, Wowta slammed the door. The sharp thorns stabbed him and in a short time he was dead.

Later, Wowta and Boona buried Tiger. When they finished, Wowta said, "Look here, Boona. I killed Tiger for you. In repayment, I want you to live with me. I'm getting old and I want someone to help with the housework."

Boona agreed to this, and she and Haburi lived with Wowta from then on. While the old witch prepared magical charms for people, Boona cooked meals, collected firewood and cultivated a small garden near the house. She took care of her baby and hoped that some day he would grow up to be a strong, handsome man like his father had been.

11
The Legend of Haburi

One morning, Boona went to her farm to collect cassava while Wowta remained at home to look after Haburi. However, the old witch had other plans. Using her magic powers, she changed Haburi into a young man.

"You will be my slave," she told him.

When Boona returned home in the afternoon, she could not find the baby. All she saw in the house were Wowta and a young man. She did not know he was her son.

"Where's Haburi?" Boona asked Wowta.

"Maybe he crept outside while I was resting," the old witch said casually. "Someone must have carried him away. Never mind. Here's a young man I found. He'll be my slave."

Boona looked at the young man, who stared back at her. Because of the magical change he had gone through, he did not know that she was his mother.

Boona searched for her baby everywhere, but she could not find him. She cried bitterly but did not want to quarrel with Wowta over her carelessness, because she feared that the witch would harm her.

From then on, Wowta sent Haburi on daily hunting trips. He always returned with much game, but the old witch made sure that Boona got the smallest birds or animals. Wowta always took the best for herself.

During his hunting trips Haburi took time off to swim in the rivers. Soon, he became friends with the *water-dogs* that lived in the rivers. He always looked forward to his daily swim with them.

One afternoon, as he rested on the riverbank after a long swim, an old water-dog came beside him and said, "Young man, there's something important that you should know."

"What is it?" enquired Haburi.

"First, you must know that the old woman, Wowta, who sends you to hunt every day is a witch. Secondly, the woman, Boona, who lives with you is really your mother. You were only a baby a few weeks ago, but Wowta's magic changed you into a young man so you'd be her slave. Your mother doesn't know that you are Haburi, her son. She believes that her baby was lost through Wowta's carelessness," the old water-dog explained.

That evening, when Haburi returned home, he saw that Wowta gave Boona the smallest fish he brought. After they ate dinner, Wowta went to the edge of the forest to search for herbs for her magic spells.

Boona was washing the dishes. "Did you have an interesting day today?" she asked Haburi.

"Yes, I did," replied Haburi. "I met an old water-dog who told me I am Haburi, and you're my mother. He told me that Wowta changed me from a baby to a young man so I'd be her slave."

Boona was shocked at the news. Finally, she held Haburi's hand and said softly, "I believe you. Water-dogs never lie, and they always know people's secrets."

She explained how they came to be living with Wowta. "Even though she saved us from Tiger," Haburi said, "she made sure she'd make us her slaves. She's wicked. I must kill her. If I don't kill her, we'll be her slaves the rest of our lives."

Later, when Wowta returned home, Haburi and Boona pretended they did not know each other.

The next morning, Wowta told Haburi, "Today you'll cut wood in the forest. I will go with you to collect herbs."

Haburi knew that was his chance to kill the witch. While she searched for the herbs under the trees, he cut a *cookrit* palm and made it fall on her. But the heavy blow did not do anything to her since she was protected by her magic.

Still, she was angry and suspicious. "You made that tree fall on me," she shouted at Haburi.

"Yes, I did," he snapped. "I hate you for what you did to me and my mother."

"So you know my secret, do you?" laughed the witch. "Well, you'll continue to be my slave, and I'll make sure you never escape. My magic will ensure that you stay with me and return even when I send you out hunting."

Haburi knew that he could not kill the witch by ordinary means. He also made up his mind that he must attempt to escape.

His first opportunity came one day when Wowta sent him on a long journey to the Atlantic Ocean to collect crabs on the beach. When he arrived at the seashore, he collected large pieces of driftwood, and made a raft. He climbed on, and with a long pole, he pushed away from land.

"I'm free," he shouted.

As the raft sailed away, Haburi knew he had to find a magician who was more powerful than Wowta to free him and his mother from the evil witch.

Suddenly, huge waves drove his raft back to shore. He realized that his attempt to escape had failed.

"I'm sure Wowta's magic made those waves drive me back," he said.

Knowing that he had failed, he collected a *quake* of crabs and went home.

"How did you like the waves?" Wowta jeered. "I told you that you can't escape from me!"

But Haburi was determined to escape. He carefully collected wax from wild bee hives in the forest, secretly shaping a wax canoe on the riverbank. However, as soon as he pushed his canoe into the river, it suddenly burst into flames. Very rapidly, the molten wax disappeared in the water of the river.

"That has to be Wowta's work," he sighed.

Nevertheless, Haburi never gave up. He made canoes of wood, but they always disappeared just when he was ready to flee.

Wowta loved honey, and she sent Haburi to collect it from the wild bee hives in the forest. Every time he did, he hid the wax he drained. One morning the witch told him, "I don't believe you're bringing home all the honey you collect. I'm going today to see that you get all of it."

Later that day, Haburi found a hive in a hollow tree trunk near the place where he stored his wax collection. The smell of honey in the tree trunk was so appetizing that Wowta could not wait for Haburi to remove the sweet liquid. She pushed him aside and crept into the hole to drink the honey.

Haburi saw that was his chance. He hurriedly gathered his hidden wax and tightly blocked the hole, trapping Wowta inside. She tried to escape, but the hole was plugged too tightly. Even her magic failed her.

The angry bees in the hive stung her so badly that all she could do to save herself was to change herself into a frog. As a frog, she lost all her magic powers and she remained helplessly imprisoned in the tree.

Haburi quickly made a raft on which he and Boona sailed down the river and escaped from the area where Wowta lived. Eventually, the sailed into the wide Atlantic Ocean and arrived finally at another land where they lived happily without fear of the wicked witch.

As for Wowta, she remained as a frog in the hollow tree trunk. She finally escaped when the bees made a hole in the wax which blocked the entrance to the hive. As a frog she wandered in the swamps in search of her slave, Haburi. To this day, the bumps from the bee stings remain on her skin. She still hops about, shouting Haburi's name, but every time she shouts, her voice comes out as an ugly croak.

The otter, or water-dog

12
The Legend Of The Haiarri Root

Many years ago, there were many Amerindian villages on both banks of the Mazaruni River. From a very early age, the Amerindian boys and girls learned to swim in the river. Except for babies and a few toddlers, everyone in the village knew how to swim.

In one village lived a man with his three-year old son, Haiarri. One morning, the boy asked his father to take him to the river and teach him to swim. The father was happy to see his son taking an interest in swimming, so he held the boy's hand and, together, they walked to the river.

The river was always full of fish, which were either shot with arrows or trapped by the fishermen of the villages. As soon as Haiarri's father put him in the water, a very strange thing happened! Some of the fish that swam under the surface near the boy suddenly became unconscious and floated to the surface.

At first, Haiarri and his father were astounded to see the fish floating near them, but in the end they gathered them and took them home. They discovered that the fish were very fresh, and, after Haiarri's mother cleaned them, she prepared a large meal of fish for dinner.

Haiarri's father was excited. He knew the fish became unconscious when he placed his son in the water. After they ate their dinner, he told his wife, "This is a good way to catch fish. All I have to do is to put Haiarri in the river, and all the fish nearby will float to the surface where can gather them easily."

Every day, little Haiarri's father took him to the river. He quickly learned to swim, and his father collected large amounts of fish.

Because of the boy's strange gift, the fish in the river feared that all of them would soon be caught. They, therefore, called a meeting to decide how to handle the new threat to their lives. Finally, the fish decided that they would all attack Haiarri when he sat on the riverbank. This was the only time they could safely approach. If he was in the water, no fish could get near him without falling unconscious.

They kept a careful watch on Haiarri, and, one afternoon, they saw him sitting on a log near the water. In a flash, all the fish jumped out of the water and stabbed him with their fins, then plunged back into the river. The stingray's stab was the worst — it was poisonous.

"Help me, Father!" Haiarri screamed. "The stingray stabbed me!"

Rushing to Haiarri, his father saw that his little son was dying. He lifted him up in his arms and, as he was taking him home, drops of the boy's blood fell on the ground.

Then another strange thing happened. In every spot where a drop of Haiarri's blood fell, a plant grew up. That became known as the *haiarri* plant. Ever since, the Amerindians have used this plant to catch fish. All they have to do is to cut a piece of the root of the plant and place it in a stream. Soon, any fish near the root becomes unconscious and floats to the surface to be gathered by a fisherman.

13
The Man Who Liked To Boast

There once was a young man named Bhamoo. Ever since he was a boy, he loved to boast about himself, and he always liked to tell others that he was the best hunter in the land. He also bragged that there was no one stronger than he was.

One bright, sunny day, Bhamoo went to visit relatives who lived in another village. There, they introduced him to the other young men who lived in the neighborhood. These young men were friendly, and, to entertain Bhamoo, they took him on a frog hunt.

In that village, frog legs were normally used for making a tasty meal, and it was common for the young men to hunt for large frogs that lived among the tall grass on the riverbanks. Each hunter had a stout piece of wood to hit the frogs.

Bhamoo was handed a stick and told that he had to hit the frogs hard, because they were very large.

He tossed the stick away and boasted, "I don't need a weapon to kill a frog. All I have to do is jump on one and wring his neck."

The king of the frogs heard Bhamoo boast and decided to teach him a lesson. In those days, frogs understood the language of people, but they could not speak it themselves.

The king of the frogs called all the frogs that lived near his home and asked them to croak as loudly as they could, while he himself would pretend to be asleep on the river bank.

Suddenly, loud croaking began, and Bhamoo, who was really a coward, became afraid. The other young men laughed.

"Don't be afraid, Bhamoo. It's only the croaking of the frogs," they told him.

"I'm not afraid," quickly replied Bhamoo. "I just never heard so many frogs croak at once before."

Then he saw the huge king of the frogs laying on the riverbank. Wanting to impress his companions, Bhamoo jumped on the frog's back and threw his arms around its neck.

The frog spun quickly around and wrapped his legs tightly around Bhamoo's body, and plunged into the river with him. The frog kept him under the water until he thought his lungs would burst, then he brought the young man back to the surface again.

When Bhamoo's companions saw him disappear into the river they thought he drowned. But when they saw him brought up to the surface by the frog, his legs tightly wrapped around the braggart, they laughed.

Bhamoo shouted, "Don't stand there and laugh! Come and get this frog away from me."

"Wring its neck, Bhamoo!" they shouted.

The king of the frogs swam away with Bhamoo and dumped him on the opposite bank. The braggart was terribly embarrassed by the way the frog handled him, and he never returned to his relatives' village again. He never returned to his own village, either. He was afraid people would laugh at him over the way the frog carried him away.

He went far away until he found a distant village. There he married and lived to a very old age, but he never boasted about anything again and became a respectable member of the community. Whenever he heard a young man boasting, he called him aside and said, "Never boast. Be modest, and people will respect you."

14
The Young Hunter And The Magician's Daughter

Kassikaitu was a young hunter who was well-known throughout the land for his skill. Every other day, he went deep into the forest to hunt wild animals. He always returned home with a dead animal slung over his shoulders. His hunting dogs always accompanied him. They were trained to chase and catch the animals he pursued.

Nearby lived an old magician. His home was beside the pathway Kassikaitu took when he journeyed into the forest. The magician had a beautiful daughter named Rewa, who fell in love with the young hunter and dearly hoped that she would be his wife someday.

Whenever the young man returned from his hunt, Rewa stood by the pathway outside her home so that he could see her. Unfortunately, the young hunter never seemed to notice her. He seemed more concerned with the dead animal on his shoulders or his hunting dogs running beside him.

Finally, the disappointed young woman told her father of her secret love for Kassikaitu.

"My dear father, I love him very much, but he never looks at me when I stand beside the path. He's more concerned with his dogs than with anything else. Maybe, I'm not beautiful as others think.

"That's not true, Rewa. You are the most beautiful maiden among our people. I'm sure that he'll notice you someday and want to marry you," her father replied.

No matter how often she stood by the pathway for Kassikaitu to notice her, she always went home disappointed. He never looked at her.

One evening, she begged her father, "Since Kassikaitu only seems to notice his dogs, I want you to use your magic and change me into a hunting dog." Her father, who saw how much Rewa loved the hunter, agreed. He gave her a piece of animal skin, and explained, "This is a magic skin. All you have to do is place it on your shoulders, and instantly, every thing that looks at you will see you as a hunting dog."

The following morning, as Kassikaitu passed, Rewa put the magic skin around her shoulders and joined him in his hunting trip through the forest. To the others, she was just another dog.

She did not stay until the end of the hunt. As soon as the dogs chased a young deer, she slipped away and hurried out of the forest to Kassikaitu's home. There she swept the house clean, baked cassava bread for him, and went to her own home.

When Kassikaitu returned home that evening, he was surprised to find his house tidy and a meal of cassava bread waiting for him. He assumed that one of his kind neighbors came in to help him while he was away from home. "I wonder who it was?" he said.

Every other day, the magically disguised girl joined the hunter in part of the hunt, then she hurried away to do his housework before he got home.

He, in turn, always thought that one of his neighbors did it while he was away.

At her home, Rewa felt better. "At least things are a bit better now," she told her father. "I'm near my lover part of the day, even though he doesn't know. I'm glad I can prepare meals for him while he's away."

One day, as Kassikaitu and his dogs killed a deer, he realized one of his dogs was missing. It was Rewa, who slipped off as soon as the dogs began chasing the deer.

"I wonder what happened to that other dog," he thought. "Maybe it was injured while we chased the deer."

He called his dogs, threw the deer on his shoulders, and began to search for the missing dog.

He never found it. By the time he realized he was not going to

Amerindian Legends of Guyana

Amerindian house

succeed, he saw he was near his home.

"Since we're almost back, we should forget hunting any more today," he told the dogs.

As he arrived near the front door, he heard sounds inside the house. He quietly set down the deer and peeked through the window. To his surprise, he saw a beautiful young woman baking cassava bread on the fire. He immediately fell in love with her. She had to be the person who was secretly doing his chores when he was away from the house.

He rushed inside. "Who are you?"

"I am Rewa, the magician's daughter," she said quietly.

"So, you are the person who comes to do my housework? Why?

Hesitantly, Rewa replied, "I do this because I love you. I have loved you for a long time, but you never noticed me."

"I notice you now, and I love you too," Kassikaitu told her. "It was lucky for me that I was searching for a missing dog, or else you'd have been gone by the time I got back. I'd still be wondering who was the kind person doing all my chores."

Rewa smiled, "You haven't lost a hunting dog. *I* was the dog in disguise."

She explained the power of the magic skin and how she accompanied him on his hunting trips. She even put it on to show him how it worked.

"From today," Kassikaitu told her, "you don't have to come here secretly. Let's go to your father so that I can tell him that I want to marry you."

They went to Rewa's house, and her father happily welcomed his future son-in-law. They immediately began making arrangements for the wedding.

One week later, Rewa and Kassikaitu were married, and they lived happily after.

15
The Old Man's Waterfall

Once upon a time, there was a little village on the Potaro River, just above the huge waterfall now known as Kaieteur. In the region was also a large stretch of grassland. Many animals like deer and anteaters lived there, supplying the game the village men hunted. Near the village, the people cultivated farms of cassava, sweet potatoes, corn and green vegetables.

In the village was an old man named Kaie. He was a hard worker in his younger days, and he was a clever hunter and fisherman. Even though he did not like farming much, he produced good crops of cassava and corn.

But now Kaie was old, and, like so many old men who worked hard in their youth, he was senile and talked to himself as he walked slowly through the village.

No one wanted to stop and chat with him, because no one understood his words. Huge sores that refused to heal were on his feet, making them unpleasant to look at. What was worse, Kaie became a nuisance. At any time of the day or night, he would enter the home of a villager without being invited and would not leave unless asked to do so.

People complained to each other about his behavior.

"Old Kaie's disgusting," one man said. "Yesterday, some people from another village came to visit my family. Of all days, Old Kaie chose that day to walk into my home! He sat on the floor, muttering to himself, and, with those sores on his feet, you can understand how embarrassed I felt."

"I know how you feel," another man replied. "All of us are suffering from the man's disgusting behavior."

As time passed, old Kaie became a worse nuisance than

Amerindian Legends of Guyana

Kaieteur Falls

before. "Why do we have to work to provide food for him?" a young man asked. "Have you ever seen him when he eats with us? He devours more than three of us!"

Eventually, the villagers called a meeting to discuss Kaie's attitude. Everyone agreed the old man was the worst problem the village ever had.

"How can we stop him from being such a nuisance?" a young man asked.

A general discussion developed over the methods to be used. Some suggested that they should send Kaie away from the village by force, but others disagreed.

"If we do that," they said, "he'll go to another village and pester the people there."

After more discussion, they finally decided to set Kaie adrift in a canoe on the Potaro River.

"He'll go over the waterfall," they reasoned. "That will be the end of the problem."

Early the next morning, Kaie was placed in a canoe with his *pegall,* a type of basket, containing everything he owned. The canoe was pushed into the speeding current of the river by two young men from the crowd of villagers who gathered on the bank. It quickly picked up speed as the raging current dragged it toward the waterfall.

Suddenly, Kaie realized his fate. "Save me! Save me!" he screamed. "I promise to be good!"

But it was too late. The canoe sped along the river, and the villagers watched in silence from the bank. Nearer and nearer the canoe drifted toward the waterfall. Old Kaie's screams rang in the air, but they were soon drowned out by the roaring water. Then, gracefully, the canoe tumbled over the mighty waterfall and disappeared.

Most likely, Kaie died, but his body was never found by the men who went to the foot of the waterfall to make sure that he was dead. A short distance downstream, they found a narrow, rocky island shaped like an upturned canoe. And, curiously, on the river bank at the foot of the waterfall was a rock shaped like Kaie's *pegall.*

"Maybe we did something wrong," one of the searchers said.

"His canoe and *pegall* turned into rocks to remind us of the wrong we did to Kaie."

Ever since, the people of the village called the waterfall Kaieteur, the waterfall of Kaie, to honor the old man.

To this day, the rock formations shaped like an upturned canoe and a *pegall* can still be seen near the foot of the Kaieteur Falls.

16
The Girl Who Was Once A Monkey

A long time ago, in the forest on the bank of the Essequibo River, an old hunter caught a young monkey and took it home for a pet. He and his old wife took good care of the monkey, and it soon became very attached to them.

The monkey came from a monkey family that knew magic, but the old hunter and his wife did not know their pet possessed such powers.

As time passed, the monkey grew to love the old couple. One day, they went into the forest to hunt birds. Shortly after they left, the monkey took off its skin and changed into a beautiful maiden. She quickly did all the household chores the old woman had not done.

After she finished preparing a meal for the old couple, she put on her monkey skin again and changed back into a monkey.

When the hunter and his wife returned from the forest, they were surprised to find all the housework finished and a meal prepared for them.

"I wonder who was so kind as to do all this?" the old woman asked.

"Maybe someone sees how old we are and came to help us while we were away," the old man suggested.

The next day, the old couple went into the forest to collect firewood. When they returned home, they again found all the chores done. They never dreamed that their pet monkey could change into a girl and do the work for them.

"It's a pity our pet monkey can't speak," the hunter said. "Then we'd know who came to help us while we were away."

Thus, the situation continued. Every time the old couple left, the monkey changed into a girl and did all the housework.

The old couple still wondered who the mysterious person was

Amerindian Legends of Guyana

Amerindian mother and child

who was helping them.

One evening when the couple returned from a fishing trip and found all the household chores finished and a meal waiting for them, the man whispered to his wife, "The next day we go into the forest, I'll ask my nephew to secretly watch the house and see who comes to do the housework for us."

The next time the hunter and his wife went into the forest to hunt, the nephew, who was a hunter, too, hid in some bushes near the house. From there, he could see into house through an open window.

The monkey thought that she was alone, so she quickly removed her skin and again changed into a beautiful girl. She picked up the broom and began sweeping the floor.

The young man, from his hiding place, saw the transformation and was shocked. When he recovered, he was even more astounded at the girl's beauty. He fell in love with her, rushed into the house, and grabbed her arm.

"Please don't change back into a monkey," he begged her. "You are a beautiful girl. I want to marry you."

She smiled. "If you promise to be kind to me, I'll marry you."

"How could I ever be unkind?" he asked. "Of course, I promise to be always kind to you."

The girl agreed to be his wife. The young man quickly picked up the monkey skin from the floor and threw it in the kitchen fire where it quickly burned to ashes.

When the old couple returned from the forest later that day, they met their nephew with the beautiful maiden. He explained to them how the monkey changed into the girl to help them, and he also told them of their plans to marry.

"I can't become a monkey again," the girl said. "My magical monkey skin was destroyed in the fire."

A few days later, they were married, and, after a while they had a son.

The girl was very hard-working and kind to her husband. At first, he was kind to her, too, but after the birth of their son, he forgot his promise. He expressed displeasure with the food she prepared and made insulting remarks about her. She became very sad, but she remained kind to her husband even when he treated her poorly.

One morning, as she held her baby son in her arms, she told her husband, "I'm taking our son to the river to bathe him."

Her husband grunted a reply. She picked up a *calabash* and left the house.

After a few hours passed, she still had not returned, so her husband left the house and went searching for her. When he arrived at the riverbank, he saw, much to his surprise, his wife walking like a monkey. The child was copying her.

"What are you doing?" he shouted as he ran up to her.

"I don't want to live with you anymore," she yelled back at him. "You treat me badly, and I want to be a monkey again."

Then he realized he had become an unkind husband.

"My wife, please forgive me," he begged her. "I'll be kind to you. Please don't leave me."

"You broke your promise once. You'll do it again," she replied.

He tried to grab her, but she leaped on a tree growing on the edge of the bank. Her baby also leaped behind her just like a monkey. As they jumped from tree to tree, her husband ran beneath them, begging her to come back.

Finally, the mother and her son reached a place where the river was narrow. On the other bank were hundreds of monkeys on the trees.

"My people!" she shouted, "I want to escape my bad husband and come back with my son."

The monkeys on the opposite bank quickly climbed a very tall tree. Their combined weight made it bend down until the girl could reach it. She held her son and jumped toward it and grasped its branches. Then she climbed down the tree and was united with her monkey relatives. Her husband was left on the opposite bank. He never saw his wife and son again.

To this day, if someone travels on the broad Essequibo River, he comes to a place where the riverbanks are close to each other. That place is still known as Monkey Jump.

17
The War Of The Birds

Long, long ago, men regarded animals as equal to human beings. All birds, beasts, and humans understood each other's language, and they lived in peace, helping each other.

In those days, Kamoa, a young man from the Rupununi Savannahs, married the daughter of King Vulture who lived in Skyland on top of Mount Ayanganna. According to the customs of those days, when a man married, he had to live at the home of his wife's parents.

Kamoa went to live on top of Mount Ayanganna at the home of his parents-in-law. There he was warmly welcomed by his wife's relatives, who were huge vultures.

After remaining with the vultures for a while, Kamoa missed his home and dearly wanted to see his relatives who lived on the savannah south of the mountain.

One day, he told his wife, "I want to visit my old home and see my relatives and friends."

"I must tell my father of your request," she replied.

Later that day, she conveyed her husband's request to her father, King Vulture.

"No!" her father said. "He can't go! "Our customs say that when someone is married to a member of the vulture family, he must never return to his parents' home."

However, Kamoa continued to insist that he must go. In the end, his wife and the other vultures became very angry with him for insisting. As a punishment, they put him to sit on top of a tall *awarra* palm. The trunk of the tree was full of sharp thorns that kept him from climbing down. He remained alone up there for many weeks.

One day, a group of spiders came to eat the ripe yellow *awarra*

Amerindian Legends of Guyana

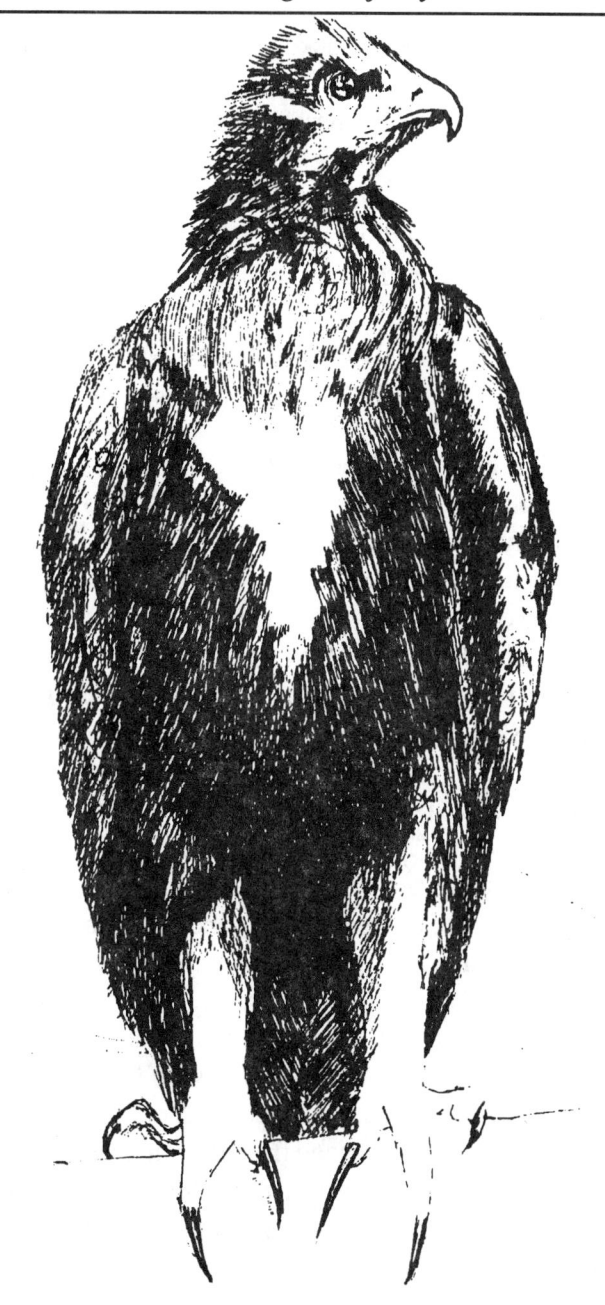

The harpy eagle

nuts on the tree. They were shocked to find Kamoa sitting among the branches.

"What are you doing here?" they asked.

He explained his quarrel with the vultures and how he was trapped in the tree. The spiders were sorry to hear about his plight. They took pity on him and spun a cord that went from the branches to the foot of the mountain. Kamoa was able to climb down and return to his parents' home.

Despite the bad treatment he received from the vultures, Kamoa loved his wife very dearly. He sent many messages with other birds, urging her to live with him in his home on the savannah. But even though she came to acknowledge that she missed him and loved him, she could not leave her parents' home and go to him.

"Tell my husband I can't come, because my relatives prevent me," she told the *harpy eagle* who brought a message from Kamoa.

Kamoa cried bitterly when he received this answer. The birds on the savannah felt pity for him and were very annoyed with the vultures. Finally, the harpy eagle told him, "All the birds have decided to take you to Skyland. We'll fight the vultures and return your wife to you."

Kamoa agreed to this plan. Early the next morning, all the birds flew to Skyland. Two huge eagles held Kamoa's arms in their beaks as they flew toward the vultures' home.

A great war of the birds took place in Skyland on the summit of Mount Ayanganna. In the end, the vultures were defeated and their homes were burned to the ground. Unfortunately, Kamoa's wife was killed by her relatives so she could not return with him. Kamoa himself was killed by his son who sided with his mother's relatives.

When the war ended, a quarrel broke out among the victorious birds over how the treasure seized from the vultures should be shared. A big fight took place between the *trumpet bird* and the *heron*. As they wrestled, they rolled in the ashes and stained their feathers. To this day, the descendants of the trumpet bird still have grey backs. Those of that particular heron are grey all over.

While the other birds watched the fight, the owl, who stayed in the background, found a small box carefully wrapped in leaves. He sneaked off with it behind some trees and opened it.

The box was full of darkness. When he opened it, the darkness quickly surrounded him. Ever since, the owl has been forced to spend its waking hours in the darkness.

The *kiskadee* did not join the other birds when they invaded Skyland. He was a coward, and he bandaged his head so he could stay at home, claiming he was ill.

When the birds eventually returned home, the hawks discovered his trickery and forced him to wear the white bandage around his head as a sign of his cowardice.

Ever since, the *kiskadee* still has a white band around his head. In his anger, he always attacks hawks whenever he sees them.

18
The Adventures Of Kororomanna

Among the Amerindians of the Warrau tribe, one of the greatest hunters was a young man named Kororomanna. One day, while hunting in the forest, Kororomanna killed a big black *baboon* by shooting it with his bow and arrow. He threw the dead baboon across his shoulder and set out for home.

The weight of the baboon slowed him down, and he was still in the forest when night fell. Nevertheless, he kept walking, but he could not see well and he became lost.

Dropping the dead baboon, Kororomanna quickly erected a *benab*, a shed made with sticks and branches. Pulling the dead animal near to him, he lay under the shelter and fell asleep.

Kororomanna built his *benab* near the road used by *hebus*. These were forest spirits that were active at night. They were normally short and hairy, and their eyebrows were long and jutted out very straight, making it impossible for them to look upward. If they had to look upward, they had to stand on their heads.

On that particular night, it seemed as if many of the *hebus* were traveling on the road. They made a lot of noise as they hurried along. The noise woke Kororomanna, and, to show his annoyance, he picked up a stout stick and struck the dead baboon's body.

By then, the body was very swollen. When Kororomanna hit it, it made a booming sound like a drum. The loud sound quickly attracted of the *hebus*. They searched for the source and found the *benab* with Kororomanna sitting under it.

Kororomanna disliked the *hebus* and was somewhat frightened of them, so he did not wait to see them enter his *benab*. He slipped away into the darkness through the back and hurriedly climbed a tall *manicole* palm tree to hide.

When the *hebus* entered the *benab*, they thought the baboon lying on the ground was the one who made all the noise.

"You were very rude to disturb us with your noise," one of the *hebus* said.

They began to beat the dead animal with sticks. It immediately sounded like a drum.

Kororomanna, who was hiding among the branches of the *manicole* tree, was very amused at the sound the swollen baboon's body made. He burst out in laughing, and the *hebus* knew something was wrong.

"This isn't the one who disturbed us." The leader pointed at the dead baboon. "This is a dead baboon. The one we're looking for is a man. He's up the *manicole* tree."

They left the dead baboon in a rush and ran to the *manicole* tree. As they gathered about it, they stood on their heads with their feet in the air, and looked up.

"There he is!" they shouted.

They saw Kororomanna still laughing, sitting among the tree branches.

"Let's cut down the tree," one of the *hebus* told the others. They immediately set to work with their axes, but they were made of turtle shells and soon broke. They then used their knives, but these were made of wood, and they broke, too. Finally, the *hebus* sent a magic rope up the tree to pull Kororomanna down. The head of the rope was that of a live snake. As soon as it reached Kororomanna, he chopped off the head with his knife. The rope lost its magical power and it fell to the ground.

The *hebus* gathered under the tree to decide what to do next. After much argument, one suggested, "Let's send the strongest of us up the tree to capture the man. As soon as he grabs the man, he must throw him down and shout, 'There is the man. Kill him quickly.'"

They all agreed to this plan, and the strongest *hebu* went up the tree. But Kororomanna, who had heard their plans very clearly, was waiting for him. When the *hebu* reached the branches, Kororomanna grabbed him and threw him down to the ground. "There is the man,"

The baboon

he shouted. "Kill him quickly!"

All the other *hebus*, who had collected stout pieces of wood, began to beat their friend. It was too dark to see who it was.

While the beating was going on, Kororomanna slipped down the tree and escaped. It was not until the *hebus* had clubbed their friend to death that they realized they had been tricked.

They ran about searching for Kororomanna, but they had to give up the search. Daylight was approaching, and they were afraid of it.

After Kororomanna escaped from the *manicole* tree, he ran for some distance through the forest. The *hebus* did not hear him because they were busy beating their friend. Nevertheless, he feared that they would search for him once they realized their mistake.

He, therefore, looked for a hiding place. At first, it was too dark to find one, but he eventually saw a big hole on a large tree trunk.

"This will make a good hiding place," he said to himself. "I can remain inside this hollow tree trunk until daylight. Then I can escape easily, because the *hebus* are afraid to move about in the daylight."

He climbed through the hole. To his surprise, he found a young woman inside the tree.

"Who are you?" the frightened woman asked.

"I'm Kororomanna, the hunter. I'm hiding from the *hebus*, who are searching for me. What are you doing here?"

"This is my home," she stated. "My husband is a huge snake, a *camudi*, and we live here. You must leave. If you don't, he will eat you when he returns.

Kororomanna did not want to leave. He was afraid the *hebus* would find him and kill him. "I'm not afraid of a snake," he told her. "I'll stay here until the *hebus* give up their search."

The young woman begged him to go, but he insisted on staying.

Just as the sun rose, the snake returned from his nightly hunt. He saw Kororomanna sitting in a corner and went up to him in a threatening manner.

"I'm going to eat you," he snarled.

At that moment, a humming bird flew past the hole on the tree trunk. Kororomanna and the snake saw it.

"That's my uncle," said Kororomanna. "If you eat me, he will certainly kill you."

"I'm not afraid of a little humming bird," declared the snake. As he spoke, a wild duck flew past.

"That's another of my uncles," Kororomanna told the snake. "If you eat me, he'll surely kill you."

"I'm not afraid of a wild duck," pointed out the snake. Then a hawk flew past.

"That hawk is also my uncle," Kororomanna said. "If you eat me, he will certainly kill you."

The snake became frightened. He knew that hawks loved to eat snakes, no matter how big they were.

"Look," he said, visibly frightened, "I won't eat you. But you have to leave right away."

Kororomanna, who was frightened of the snake, climbed out the hole in the trunk and continued his journey.

Since it was daylight, he was not afraid of the *hebus*, but he was still lost in the forest. He walked until he found a narrow path. It was not familiar, but he followed it for some time until he came to a place where a hollow tree trunk lay across the path. Peeking inside, he saw a *hebu* child. Kororomanna was worried that the *hebu* child would tell the other *hebus* that he had passed that way. To prevent that, he killed it.

He was just about to continue his journey when he heard noises in the bushes nearby. He hurriedly climbed a tree and hid among the branches. He was just barely settled among the branches when the *hebu* child's mother came out. She was frightened of the daylight, but, when she saw her dead child was dead, she forgot her fear and became very angry.

She saw Kororomanna's footprints near the trunk, but she could not follow them, because there was no sandy soil off the path. Returning to her dead child, she scooped up some sand which held one of Kororomanna's footprints and wrapped it in a large leaf. She tied it with a small vine and placed it near the hollow tree trunk. After that, she set about collecting firewood in the bushes.

Kororomanna watched her do all that as he sat in the tree. He suspected that the mother *hebu* would hurt him with magic. As soon as she moved away from the path into the tall bushes to look for more firewood, he swiftly climbed down, untied the leaf containing the sand with his footprint and, after throwing away the sand, substituted sand that had the mother's footprint. When he finished, he climbed back up the tree again.

Shortly after, the mother returned. She heaped the firewood she collected and got a big fire going. She threw the leaf containing the footprint into the fire and shouted, "I curse the one whose footprint I burn. May he fall into the fire, too."

She believed that her magic power would pull the person into the fire and kill him. It worked, but she was pulled in, not Kororomanna, and was immediately burned to ashes.

After that incident, Kororomanna continued his journey along the strange path. After following it for hours, he eventually reached a wider, clearer path and thought his journey would be easier.

As soon as he stepped on the new path, his feet stuck fast to the ground. He tried to tug himself free, but the harder he tried, the more stuck he was.

"At last," sighed Kororomanna. "This is the end. I can't escape. This is a magical trap set by the *hebus*. I wonder how I can escape this."

He threw himself on the ground and pretended to be dead. Ants swarmed across him, stinging savagely, but he never moved. The clear path was a magical fish and animal trap set by the *hebus* who lived in the area. As night fell, a group of *hebus* came to see what they caught. When they saw Kororomanna stuck there, they thought they caught a large fish.

The *hebus* released Kororomanna from the magical trap and placed him on the ground near the path. All this time, he still pretended to be dead and remained limp.

"Let's take it to the river and wash it," one *hebu* said. "See how it is covered with ants and dust?"

"We don't have a basket to fetch it," another said.

"Let's find some vines to make a basket," said the first one. "Then we can put the big fish inside and take it to the river to wash it."

All agreed, and they hurried off among the bushes to search for vines. With no one watching him, Kororomanna jumped up and ran away.

He continued his wandering but he still could not find the path that led from the forest to his home.

Early one morning, when it was still dark, he arrived at a clearing in which he saw a deep pond. On the bank was a *hebu* trying to empty the water with a little *calabash* bowl.

Kororomanna knew that if the *hebu* saw him, his life would be in danger.

He decided to kill the *hebu*. He fired two arrows into the *hebu's* back, but the *hebu* did not seem to feel them. The *hebu* though they were flies and brushed them away with his hands.

When a third arrow struck him, he turned and saw Kororomanna, who rushed toward the bushes to escape, only to trip on a vine and fall on his face.

The *hebu* was on him in a flash. He dragged Kororomanna near to the pond and imprisoned him in a hollow tree trunk.

"When I'm finished emptying water from the pond, I'll kill you," the *hebu* said.

Kororomanna was terrified. "Please don't kill me," he begged. "If you spare my life, I'll give you beautiful rattles."

"I don't want rattles," said the *hebu*.

"I'll give you lots of *paiwarri* if you spare me," Kororomanna begged again.

"I don't want any *paiwarri*. I don't use any alcoholic drinks," declared the *hebu*. "Don't bother me. I'll kill you when I finish my work of emptying the pond."

Kororomanna made a final plea. "Please don't kill me. I'll give you some tobacco if you set me free."

All *hebus* loved tobacco. He quickly released the hunter from the tree trunk. "Where is the tobacco?" he demanded.

Luckily, Kororomanna had some in a little bag tied to his belt. He handed it to his captor, who was delighted by such a valuable gift. He chewed some for a while, then said, "You're the first man to give me tobacco. From now on, we will be friends."

"I prefer to be your friend instead of your enemy," replied Kororomanna.

"What's your name?" asked the *hebu*.

"My name is Kororomanna. What's yours?"

"I'm Huta Kurakura."

Thus, Kororomanna and Huta Kurakura became friends.

"Why are you emptying the pond?" Kororomanna asked.

"This pond has a lot of fish. It will be easier to catch them without the water," explained Huta Kurakura.

Kororomanna helped him to empty the water from the pond. Later, they collected the large amount of fish which Huta Kurakura divided into two large heaps.

"One is yours," he told Kororomanna.

Kororomanna pointed out, "I won't be able to take so many fish home."

"That's no problem." He used his magic to tie Kororomanna's share in a small, leaf-covered bundle. "All your fish are in here. Follow the path that leads away from the pond, and you'll find your way home."

After saying farewell to Huta, Kororomanna picked up his tiny bundle and followed the pathway. Eventually, he saw he was on a familiar trail that would lead him to his home.

Finally, he arrived home where his wife and mother were wondering what happened to him since he had been missing for many days. They were very happy to see him.

After he told them of his adventures, he showed them the little bundle. "I brought a lot of fish for you."

The two women laughed when they saw the little bundle.

"How could such a tiny thing hold a lot of fish?" his mother asked in disbelief.

Kororomanna untied the tiny bundle. So many fish came out of it that the house was filled from the floor to the roof. Kororomanna, his wife and mother had to rush outside because there was no room left for them in the house.

They invited all the people of the village to take as many fish as they wanted. Finally, they were able to get back into their house. For weeks afterward, fish was the meal of all the people of Kororomanna's village.

19
The Origin Of The Calabash

The Arawak people enjoyed long periods of happiness in the past, but there were times when they endured great sufferings, too. There was one period when all bad things seemed to happen to them. It started with a period of heavy rainfall that lasted for weeks. Rivers rose and flooded the countryside. Soon, even the soil of the farmlands was washed away.

Then the rain stopped. Since the flood destroyed all the crops, there was very little food available. Then animals the Arawaks hunted had moved to the distant mountains to escape the rising waters. And even when the Arawaks planted crops again, the plants died, because the soil was too thin to sustain them.

The result was a great famine. Great hunger stalked the land. Various illnesses affected the people, too. Every day, the Arawaks mourned the deaths of children, young adults and old people. Women wailed over the deaths of loved ones while men silently wondered how the times of abundant food and no disease could ever return.

Among the Arawaks was a *piaman* named Arawanili. He tried his charms and magic in an effort to drive away suffering from the land, but all his efforts failed.

"You're no longer a worthy *piaman*," people rebuked him. "Your charms and magic are weak. We don't need you if you can't help us."

Arawanili was very sad to see his people suffer. He understood why everyone was angry with him. They rejected him out of frustration, but he was even more sad when he saw they had no hope.

Early one morning, Arawanili sat on the riverbank, thinking of the hardships his people endured. As he gazed on the river's quiet water, a female water spirit suddenly rose out from it. Arawanili jumped in surprise.

"Don't be afraid, Arawanili," the water spirit said. "My name is Orehu. I want you to help your people overcome their misery and suffering."

"But they have rejected me," replied Arawanili. "They say that I'm not a worthy *piaman*."

"They are frustrated by all their suffering. They aren't responsible for their words."

"How can I help remove the misery and suffering we face?"

"Let me explain," Orehu pointed out. "Your magic, like that of all *piamen*, is weak against the evil spirits that bring things like famine and disease. You need something new to use against those spirits."

From under the water, Orehu pulled a branch bearing light-green leaves. She handed it to Arawanili. "Plant this. When it bears fruits, pick two and meet me at this place. Only then will I be able to show you how to help your people. I'll be watching for you."

Orehu then dived under the water and disappeared.

Arawanili took the branch home and planted it in his yard. After many months it grew into a small, shady tree. In a while, it bore large green gourds.

One morning, he picked two gourds and went to the riverbank. He barely sat down when Orehu rose from the water and climbed up the bank to sit beside him. She took the gourds from him and examined them.

"This gourd is known as *calabash*," she explained. "It will be very useful to the people. The outer skin becomes a hard shell. After the soft inner parts are removed, the *calabash* can be made into bowls, water containers, and other useful things."

Orehu cut one of the gourds into two halves with a sharp knife, then she scraped out the soft white kernel and made two neat bowls from the gourd halves. Then she took the other gourd and bored two holes in it at the top and the bottom. Through those, she removed the inner kernel until the gourd was hollow. She placed a few white pebbles in the hollow gourd, then put a stick through the holes, leaving

Maracas

part of the stick out for a handle. She grasped the handle and shook the gourd, which now made a rattling sound.

"This is a *maraca*," she said. "You can make it more beautiful by tying feathers to the handle. When you shake it, the rattling will chase away the evil spirits that are bringing suffering to your people." She handed it to him and watched as he shook it.

"Shake the *maraca* whenever you practice your charms," Orehu said. "Good times will come again."

Orehu got ready to dive into the river, then she gave Arawanili a reminder. "Remember to use the *calabash* properly. No part must be wasted. Even the kernel that is dug out from it can be used for curing sores and cuts. Rub the kernel on the affected parts of the body."

Orehu plunged into the river and disappeared.

Arawanili returned home and began practicing his charms again. This time, he used his *maraca* to make loud rattling sounds which chased away the evil spirits.

Soon, the crops began to grow again, and the sick people regained their strength. Happiness again reigned over the land.

The *calabash* became one of the most useful possessions of the people. They used it for making bowls, water containers, and *maracas*. At first, *maracas* were used only by the *piamen*, but they were later adopted by musicians, and, eventually, became very popular musical instruments.

20

The Story Of Amalivacar

Long ago, shortly after the end of the first great flood, a young man, wearing a majestic, beautiful headdress, paddled his canoe up the Essequibo River. He made a long journey from a land far across the sea, and he was tired. He planned to make his home on the land near to this great river, but he wanted to travel over this new land before making a decision where to settle. His name was Amalivacar.

Although the flood waters had drained from the land, the rivers were still heavily flooded. Their waters reached far up the valley sides. As Amalivacar paddled his canoe up the rivers, he thought that it would be wise to mark his passage. He used a large diamond to scratch large drawings of people, animals and strange shapes on the rock walls at different points along the rivers. He also made drawings on many outcrops of rock that stuck up from the rivers.

Later, when the water level went down to normal, Amalivacar's drawings remained on the rocks, now high above the river level. As time passed, the Amerindians called these drawings *timehri*, or rock drawings. They can still be seen in the upper courses of the many rivers in Guyana.

One day, Amalivacar arrived at an Amerindian village on the bank of the Cuyuni River. He noticed that some men were planting some sticks on a patch of ground.

"What are you planting?" Amalivacar asked.

"We're planting arrow cane reeds. We'll use them to make good arrows," a man replied.

"But why do you need so many arrows?"

"We need them to either make war against others or to defend ourselves," another man told him.

Amalivacar became angry. "Why should you make war against

Timeheri — rock paintings and carvings

other people?" he asked. "Don't you see you're wasting your time? Rather than planting arrow cane reeds for arrows, why don't you cultivate cassava, sweet potatoes, corn and other fruits?"

The men stopped planting and crowded around Amalivacar who tied up his canoe and stood on the river bank.

"You seem to have sensible thoughts, stranger," a man said. "Why don't you stay with us and show us how to cultivate more crops?"

Some of the men were, by this time, admiring Amalivacar's canoe.

"How is it that your canoe is so well-shaped and smooth inside?" a young man asked. "We use axes to hollow our canoes, but they are not so nicely beautifully shaped as yours."

"I used fire to hollow mine," Amalivacar replied. "If you're willing to learn, I'll teach you how."

He stayed at the village for a few months, during which time he taught the people to properly cultivate food crops. He also showed them how to make canoes by using fire to hollow them.

Finally, he was ready to continue his travels. "You have new knowledge," he told them. Knowledge isn't to be locked up. You must share it with others, so that they know the good things you know."

The people obeyed him. Soon, the things Amalivacar taught were known to all the people in the region.

Amalivacar left the village and visited many others in various parts of the country, teaching and assisting people. By then, he was so well-known that his fame preceded him. He had also displayed the magical powers he possessed to help some villages. People eagerly looked forward to seeing him.

At a village in the Mazaruni River area, the residents asked, "Amalivacar, we use the river a lot to travel. It's very difficult to paddle our canoes against the current. Please use your magic to make the river flow downriver on one side and upriver on the other. That will make it easy for us to paddle in any direction."

Always eager to please, tried to comply, but no matter how much magic he used, he could not make the current flow upstream.

"This is because too much rain falls in the Pakaraima Mountains," he reasoned. "The steady rain fills the rivers, and the water constantly rushes to the sea."

Still, he had to show the people some result, or they would lose faith in him.

"I am going to the great wide sea for a while," he told them. "When I return, there will be a two-way flow of the current."

On his arrival at the sea off the mouth of the Essequibo River, he used his magic to create the tides. As a result, the water of the sea rushed up the rivers for a great distance during high tide, which made at least part of the river flow upstream. At low tide the current flowed normally.

When he returned to the village, the people were pleased. "The current goes upriver part of the day," they said. "That is very helpful."

Shortly after, Amalivacar traveled through the Potaro, Siparuni and Rupununi Rivers, spreading knowledge everywhere. Eventually, he came to the plains of Maita where he made his home in a large cave. There he relaxed by playing soothing music on instruments that he made.

Outside his cave was a large rock he hollowed. He used it as a drum to make music. To this day, the hollow rock still stands outside the cave on the Maita plains, and Amerindians in that area call it the drum of Amalivacar.

Many people went to Amalivacar's home to meet him and seek knowledge. He taught them to use herbs to cure sickness and showed them how to use the stars to guide them when they traveled at night.

As time passed, and Amalivacar grew older, he saw that the people had learned all he wanted them to know.

"My mission in this land is over," he said. "It's time for me to leave you."

Early one morning, an old grey-haired Amalivacar paddled his canoe away from his home. On the bank of the river stood a silent group of people who came to say farewell. With a final wave, Amalivacar steered his canoe around a bend of the river. The silent group saw him no more.

He paddled his canoe down the mighty Essequibo River and finally reached the broad Atlantic Ocean. Into the ocean he sailed, hoping to reach a new land where he would meet people with whom he would share his knowledge.

Glossary

Awarra - A common palm found near to Amerindian villages. It bears small, yellow fruit, which is eaten with great relish. The kernel of the round seed is used for making oil.

Baboon - A red howling monkey whose howls are very loud.

Balata - A form of natural rubber obtained from the sap of the bullet-wood tree.

Balata bleeders - Men who tap the bullet-wood tree for balata.

Benab - A small tent-like shelter made of palm leaves and sticks. It is often constructed by Amerindians when they are on long fishing and hunting expeditions.

Calabash - A large green gourd, the fruit of the calabash tree. The outer skin of the gourd becomes hard as it ages. When it is cut into two equal parts and the inner white material is removed, two strong bowls are produced. Each of these bowls is called a calabash.

Camudi - A large snake that measures a maximum of ten meters in long and one meter in circumference at its thickest part. There are two types of camudi — the land camudi, known as the boa constrictor, and the water camudi, which frequents swamps and rivers.

Casareep - A thick treacle-like liquid obtained after the juice of the bitter cassava is boiled for a long time. It can be stored for long periods and is used for the preparation of the famous Amerindian dish, pepper-pot.

Cassava - The elongated tuberous root of the cassava or manioc plant.

Cassava bread - When the juice from the grated cassava is removed, the dry cassava meal is broken in a sieve. After it is sifted, it becomes a coarse flour. Some of the flour is placed on a circular stone, or a circular flat piece of iron over a fire, where it is flattened and rounded. This is the cassava bread. After one side of it is baked, it is turned over for the other side to be cooked. When done, the cassava bread is thrown on the thatched roof of the house to dry in the sun. Once dried, it keeps for weeks.

Casseri - A pink, pleasant tasting alcoholic drink made from sweet potatoes and sugar cane. Sometimes, a small amount of cassava is added. It is prepared by boiling the ingredients and leaving them to ferment.

Cookrit - A palm tree that abounds in the interior of Guyana. The outer flesh of its fruit is very tasty. The kernel of the seed is used to make oil.

Crabwood - A big tree which grows to over twenty-five meters in height. Its timber produces a very strong, dark brown wood. The tree bears a nut from which an unpleasant-smelling oil known as crab-oil is extracted.

Curare - A poison extracted from the bark of a creeping plant known as *urari*. The Amerindians call the poison *ourali*. This poison is smeared onto arrow heads and darts for blow pipes. If the poison is smeared on an arrow which is kept warm and dry, it can retain its effectiveness for several years.

Cutlass - Before iron and steel implements became known to the Amerindians, the cutlass was made of stone. As with the modern tool, it was a slightly curved sword, with only one edge being sharp.

Farine - Cassava-meal which has had the juice removed is dried on a flat circular stone or piece of iron on a slow fire. It is not allowed to stick together, and, after a while, it resembles dry brown crumbs. These crumbs are known as farine. Farine forms an important ingredient in the Amerindian meals.

Haiarri - A small plant, the roots of which produce narcotic juices. Amerindians fish by placing pieces of the roots, which are first crushed, in small streams near to a temporary dam. Fish are rendered unconscious by juices from the roots.

Harpy eagle - The largest eagle in the world. It is now very rare and is an endangered species. Its natural habitat is in the Pakaraima and Kanuku Mountains of Guyana.

Hebus - A type of mischief-making forest spirits. Some are noted for their kindness to humans.

Heron - A medium-sized bird found in swampy areas along the banks of rivers. Most of them are white in color, but there are some which are red, pink, blue or gray. The gray heron is slightly smaller than the other species.

Hima-heru - A small plant that grows in the interior of Guyana. It is claimed that when two pieces of its dry branches are rubbed together, they catch afire very quickly.

Iguana - A large green lizard which lives among the branches of trees. It is hunted for its flesh which, when cooked, is a delicacy.

Kiskadee - A small yellow and black bird with a band of white feathers around its head.

Lukanani - A fish which lives in the smaller rivers of Guyana. It attains a length of about one meter when fully grown.

Manicole - A tall palm which grows in the interior of Guyana.

Matapee - A pliable basket-work cylinder used by Amerindians for squeezing out the juice from the grated cassava. It is about two meters long and fifteen centimeters in diameter.

Paiwarri - An alcoholic drink which is most popular among Amerindians. It is made from thick cassava bread which is specially baked until it is dark brown. This is then broken into little pieces and placed in a large pot filled with water. In the past, the large pieces were chewed by women and later replaced in the pot. That method is no longer in use. When the pot is filled, it is stirred. After a period of slight boiling, the contents are left to ferment for a few days. Sometimes, sugar cane juice is added. The result is a brown alcoholic drink.

Pegall - A basket-like container, either rectangular or round, with a cover which is of the same shape as the bottom or basket section. It is used for keeping personal items, such as clothing.

Pepper-pot - A most popular dish made by boiling meat or fish with hot pepper and casareep.

Piaman - An Amerindian medicine man. He acts as doctor, fortune-teller, rainmaker, spellbinder and dream interpreter. He is also a teacher, preacher and counselor. He is generally highly respected.

Powis - Also known as the *curassow*, this bird lives in the forest. It is as large as a turkey, and is generally black in color, with a yellow beak and legs. It is hunted for its meat.

Quake - A round, basket-like container used by fishermen to keep their catch.

Tapir - A medium-sized animal that lives in the forests of Guyana. It has very thick skin and a long snout and somewhat resembles a large pig. It is also known as *kama*, bush cow or bush donkey.

Tiger - All large members of the cat family that live in Guyana's forests are called tigers, even though no tiger actually exists in the country. The smaller species are often referred to as tiger cats. Generally, what is called a tiger is the large spotted jaguar.

Timber grants - Areas in the forests where timber is cut commercially.

Timehri - An Amerindian word which refers to the drawings and engravings found on rocks, especially near waterfalls, on the rivers in Guyana's interior.

Trumpet-bird - This smallish bird is also known as the *warracaba*. It is light gray in color, with deep, purple-black feathers on its throat and neck. It utters a deep sound similar to that of a trumpet.

Vaqueros - Cowboys who work on the cattle ranches of the Rupununi savannahs.

Warrampa - A basket-like cover.

Water-dog - The Guyanese name for an otter.

Further Reading

1. Brett, William H. *The Indian Tribes of Guiana.* (1882).

2. im Thurn, Everard F. *Among the Indians of Guiana.* (1883); republished by Dover Publications Inc: New York, 1967.

3. Lambert, Leonard. *Guiana Legends.* Roffey and Clark: London, 1931.

4. Roth, Walter E. *An Inquiry into the Animism and Folklore of the Guiana Indians.* (1915).